T0131774

Now is the time to do what you love

HOW TO MAKE THE CAREER MOVE THAT
WILL CHANGE YOUR LIFE

Nancy Whitney-Reiter

Adams Media
New York London Toronto Sydney New Delhi

Adams Media
An Imprint of Simon & Schuster, Inc.
57 Littlefield Street
Avon, Massachusetts 02322

For information about special discounts for bulk purchases, please contact Simon & Schuster Special Sales at 1-866-506-1949 or business@ simonandschuster.com.

The Simon & Schuster Speakers Bureau can bring authors to your live event. For more information or to book an event contact the Simon & Schuster Speakers Bureau at 1-866-248-3049 or visit our website at www. simonspeakers.com.

Manufactured in the United States of America

10 9 8 7 6 5 4 3 2 1

Library of Congress Cataloging-in-Publication Data has been applied for.

ISBN 978-1-6055-0052-2

For Greg,
Because the only thing better than going after your dreams
is to do so holding hands with the one you love.

ACKNOWLEDGMENTS

Thank you to my agent, Gina Panettieri, and to the team at Adams Media for this special opportunity. A thousand thanks to my father, Frank R. Spatt, for his eagle-eyed proofreading skills and no-holds-barred critiques. I'd be lost without you.

I am also indebted to the countless people who shared their stories—not just the good parts, but their failures too—so that readers would be both inspired and well-informed: Sunny Schlenger, Tom Collopy, Mary Frische, Teresa Spatt, Harry Crisp, Padre Dave, Carla Lucente, Stacy Jackowski, Jeff Gallen, John Gallen, Paul Sullivan, Larry Siegler, Maura Conry, Beth Carrigan, Adrienne Van Doren, Joanne Connors, Joemy Wilson, Barbarann Kanute, and my brother George Spatt. To the rest who chose anonymity, you have my heartfelt thanks.

Please visit the companion website:
www.unplugyourhead.com/dowhatyoulove
for a free Master Checklist and comprehensive Resource Guide!

Contents

INTRODUCTION

By the time I'd hit thirty, I'd achieved exactly the level of success that I'd spent my early adult life striving for. As a manager for a D.C.-based nonprofit trade association, I was earning a decent salary, had excellent benefits, and had just had the heady experience of delivering a presentation before Congress. As if that weren't enough, my last major project had been splashed across the pages of the *Wall Street Journal*. "See? What I'm doing is *important*," I'd say to my family and friends. I had a beautiful condo, a wide social circle, and it seemed the sky was the limit for my future achievements.

September 11, 2001, changed all of that. As it happened, I'd been attending an economics conference in the Marriott World Trade Center, where I'd also been staying. As the building came crashing down around me, so did the foundation upon which I'd built my life. I didn't know it then, but my experiences that day would forever alter my perception of success and happiness. As I made my way through the panicked crowds, engulfed by debris and smoke, I realized that all of the accolades, all of my achievements, truly meant nothing. I remember thinking, "I can't die yet . . . I haven't *lived*."

I soon moved away from D.C. and found a similar job in San Antonio, Texas. When it became clear that changing venues wouldn't solve my problems, I changed relationships. My pattern repeated itself until I realized that neither location nor outside influences had the power to change my life. My happiness, it seemed, was up to me.

As I would later write about in *Unplugged: How to Disconnect from the Rat Race, Have an Existential Crisis, and Find Meaning and Fulfillment*, I set off on an international travel sabbatical. First, I had to figure out what it was that I truly loved. Then, I promised myself, I would spend my life doing it.

As I traveled the world, I made an astounding discovery: there were people of all ages, backgrounds, and nationalities who felt *exactly* the same way I did! I'd never before met so many people who were burning out in their mid-twenties. Spurred on since their early teens to meet society's definition of "success," they had managed to climb to its pinnacle only to be confronted by an abyss of emptiness.

I met dozens of people determined to remake their lives: some I'd only meet in passing for a few hours, others I'd get to know for a week or two at a time as we worked together on various volunteer projects. I learned what makes a successful career-changer, which pitfalls to avoid, and became exposed to career paths and ideas I never would have encountered had I not set off on my own journey.

Upon my return to the United States, I began living out the life that I knew would make me happiest. I have three passions: travel, teaching, and writing, and I shrugged off the security of another corporate career to embrace a sometimes rocky, sometimes exuberant, new life.

It wasn't long before I was teaching, seeing my writing in print, and satisfying my need to travel through my work with Global Vision International, a British conservation company specializing in long-term volunteer travel experiences. I had volunteered with them during my sabbatical and had recognized their need for a U.S. branch. In less than a year after my return from my travels, I'd set up GVI USA, and began a fulfilling period in which I helped literally hundreds of people, of all ages, take extended trips and embark on their own personal journeys.

The pattern I had witnessed during my own travels now became glaringly evident through the hundreds of calls to our toll-free number. Not all of those who called ended up booking a trip: some just wanted to discuss the *possibility* of escape. "So many people want out of their lives," I thought. I heard a little of myself in all of their voices: those just graduating from college, fearful they'd make the wrong choice. Those in their thirties, unfulfilled despite outward success. And increasingly, Baby Boomers: not quite ready to retire, but not sure if they were "too old" to start over and live the life they really wanted.

It occurred to me that most of us spend our entire adult lives with one ultimate goal: achieving some degree of outwardly defined "success." We work hard, often spending long hours away from those we love, sacrificing our hobbies and interests. In our quest to reach the appropriate milestones, we willingly sacrifice our todays for a tomorrow that may never come. For too many, this means remaining in a career that no longer fulfills us. We remain planted on a never-ceasing treadmill, eventually counting the days until retirement, our eyes fixed firmly on our future success.

But how do *you* define "success?" Does it involve having multiple cars, a nice home, the latest gadgets? Does your definition involve the recognition of others: your peers, your mentors, or your family?

Or does it involve the feeling of satisfaction you have every day when you go to bed, knowing that you are spending your time (and your life) doing something you truly enjoy?

More and more people are revising their perceptions of what it means to be successful to the latter definition. They are making each minute of their life count, as opposed to counting the minutes when they can start living. They are going to bed satisfied and waking up hopeful. They are realizing that success is not a summit you reach after a lifetime of climbing, but a feeling you experience *daily* when you're doing what you love.

Right now, you are holding in your hands the culmination of my seven-year study on successful career changes. This book is a compendium of countless interviews with both armchair escapists and those who have broken through the barriers to personal fulfillment, as well as portions of my own journey. Inside these pages are the keys to empower you to step off of the treadmill and onto the path to your dream job. After all, *now* is the time to do what you love!

PART ONE

Gearing Up for the Change

So you've thought about making a career change. In fact, you've thought about it enough to move beyond thinking to your first action: picking up this book. The fact that you didn't choose a work of fiction shows that you don't want to temporarily *escape* your current life; you want to *transform* it. Now it's time to take that desire for transformation and turn it into reality.

Television and the media are full of stories of people—just like you—who have left their old lives behind and are living their dreams. Perhaps you've seen these stories; perhaps you've even felt a little envy. The truth is, there is no reason that you too can't live your dream. All you need to achieve this type of success are two things: desire and a well-executed plan.

You've brought the first element to the table; this book will walk you through the rest. Part 1, Gearing Up for the Change, will tackle the hardest part of your plan: getting a good grip on the realities of both your current situation and those of your "dream job." By the time you finish this portion of the book, you'll have an accurate assessment of whether you're truly ready for a change, and if not, exactly what you need to do to get there.

CHAPTER 1

Why Now?

Are you tired of waiting for happiness? Are you ready to step outside your comfort zone and consider a career other than the one you're in now? What about the dream you've always had to open a small business? Or perhaps you'd like to turn your hobby into something you do every day—and make money for? Like so many of us, you may have asked yourself, "What am I doing with my life?" Life's daily entanglements make it easy for our dreams to slip away; we're concerned about paying the mortgage, having health insurance, and providing security for the family. But you don't have to sacrifice a lot to go after your goals. You've come to this book because you want something more from life. And if now's the time— for you—to make those most important first steps, you'll know it after reading this chapter.

You're at a Physical Advantage

Whether you are a recent college graduate or a middle-age parent with grown children, the bitter truth is you are younger today than you ever will be in the future. Your age, whatever it is, is just one reason why you should act now to fulfill your dreams.

Your Energy

Let's start with the most apparent of reasons: You're likely to be more physically fit today than you will be at any other point in your life. If you're waiting for retirement to act, this is a given. If you're young enough to just be starting out, this may be less obvious. Even if your goal is to make the switch while you're "still young," you'll need to consider the role future responsibilities will play in your energy level (the pressures of paying a mortgage, having kids, other family obligations, etc.).

This is important when you consider the energy involved in a career change. You might have to make some serious decisions that require lots of energy. For example, you may have to get additional schooling (college or technical), relocate to where the opportunities are, sell your current home and downsize, and network, network, network! If all of that sounds daunting today, seriously consider how another ten or twenty years will impact your energy levels. By at least beginning on the path to your dream, you'll prevent yourself from wearing down faster, later on.

Employer/Customer Perceptions

Unfortunately, studies show that older people often have a harder time getting a job. This is true whether you are looking for an office job or wanting to participate in a long-term political campaign. If you are a middle-ager and competing against a bunch of twenty-somethings, the potential employer might feel compelled to go with someone who can commit to the company for a longer period of time, or who could bring more enthusiasm—not to mention fewer expectations—to the table.

The same concept is true of your future clients. If your desired career involves face-to-face contact with the public, you should be aware that your physical appearance influences how others perceive you. As we'll see in Chapter 5, people are likely to make snap judgments about your trustworthiness and intelligence based on whether you are overweight or unkempt!

If you're not in the best physical condition possible today, now is the time to start! Many employers these days offer programs to help their employees quit smoking, lose weight, and engage in other healthy lifestyle activities. Prior to leaving your current employer, make sure you've maximized these types of benefits so that you can start your new career in the best shape of your life.

Now that you've read a bit about how age can affect one's decision to change careers, consider it on a personal level. Answer the following questions in this . . .

REALITY CHECK

- What are the physical challenges associated with my desired career change?
- Can I handle them today? Will I be able to handle them tomorrow?
- Do I need to lose weight, get fit, or stop smoking?
- Does my current employer offer programs I could be taking advantage of?

You Have a Financial Advantage

Regardless of your age, there are several reasons that you may be at a financial advantage today when it comes to pursuing your career change. Since career changes can involve either an up-front investment or sacrificing current income (or in some cases, both), it pays to carefully evaluate your financial footing.

You Know Where You Stand Now

One reason to start implementing your career change plan now is that today, your financial picture is more concrete. As stated earlier, a career change can involve multiple expenses: going back to school, relocating, licenses, networking organizations, supplies, promotions for a new business, etc. Starting to plan for and implement these items into your current budget will be far easier than having to guess what your income will be like in the future, or, if you're close to retirement, living off your fixed income.

Don't make the common mistake of overestimating what your future net worth and income will be. One of easiest ways for this to happen is to consider your home as your primary investment, a common misperception among Boomers and younger generations. As illustrated by the housing bust in 2008, the economic cycle is ultimately unpredictable, which brings us to the next point.

You Can't Predict Outside Forces

Economic shocks such as natural disasters (Katrina), terrorism (9/11), war (Iraq), or financial crises (the sub-prime debacle) make it extremely difficult to paint an accurate picture of the future. The truth is, there is no way to forecast what our economy will look like in ten to twenty years, let alone if we've adequately prepared for it. There are numerous outside factors that have the potential to derail your investment train—no matter now prudent you've been or how solid your investment choices.

Just ask those who have witnessed the value of their homes decrease by a third, or their mutual fund values fall by half, despite doing everything "right." Responsible homeowners who were not in over their heads with adjustable-rate loans still ended up feeling the pinch of the subprime mortgage crash. The repercussions went on to collapse not only the domestic housing market, but the global economy as well. What began as bad decision-making by lending institutions in a few major U.S. cities ultimately affected housing prices and production as far away as Asia. With today's interwoven global economy, the same thing could potentially happen again: this time with the roots of the crisis originating elsewhere, and far off of your radar.

Benefits with Your Current Employer

Given our tendency to overestimate our assets and underestimate our costs and the general unpredictability of the economy, it makes sense to try to reduce the cost side of the equation as much as possible while you're still employed in your present job. One way to do this is to factor in benefits from your current employer. If you're lucky enough to have tuition assistance with your current employer, it's a great idea to use it! Think of the opportunities it affords you. Even if you are changing fields entirely, there may be some potential for overlap. If you need to get a degree, there may be some general education requirements that you can start on while you are still employed.

Naturally, you'll want to investigate your employer's policies carefully in terms of what they expect in return. On the positive side, however, most tuition assistance programs require an up-front commitment (a minimum tenure of three months to a year) rather than a back-end obligation (requiring you to stay for a period of time after your schooling). When you consider that the average cost per credit hour for a graduate degree is upwards of $200, going back to school today may alleviate significant financial pressure tomorrow.

Now that you've read a bit about how finances play an important role in changing careers, consider it on a personal level. Answer the following questions in this . . .

REALITY CHECK

- What costs are associated with my desired career change?
- Will there be licenses or further schooling required?
- Does my current employer have programs that will help defray the cost?
- Will I have to move?
- What do I expect my future income to be? How can I be sure it's realistic?

Your Risk Is Diminished

As any good financial advisor will tell you, the proportion of your financial portfolio involving the greatest risk should be highest in your younger, working years and lowest as you approach retirement. This concept applies equally to switching careers, and it involves two distinct types of risk.

Financial Risk: Maximizing Earnings

Statistically speaking, your early forties have been proven as the best time to change careers or go back to school. By the time you've reached middle age, you've likely acquired both a solid education as well as a track record in your line of work. As a result, middle age is the peak earning period for most adults. If you are able to make your career change prior to reaching middle age, you have a significantly greater chance of earning more money in your new career.

However, the longer you wait to make the change, the greater your difficulty in finding employment. According to a Census Bureau report, unemployment peaks as one gets older, topped by people ages forty-five to fifty-four. This is because older workers find themselves in competition for jobs with those possessing more current job skills, greater willingness to relocate and lower salary requirements.

You might be wondering, "So when is the cutoff? At what point is it too late?" Well, according to some studies on LifeTwo.com—a site dedicated to midlife improvement—the turning point in your desirability as a job candidate is right around your fiftieth birthday. This is the so-called "career cliff" where it becomes impossible to recover both your prestige and your previous salary if you're making a career switch.

If you're over fifty, don't panic! This doesn't mean that you are too old to make the change, but merely that you'll likely be sacrificing financial compensation for career satisfaction. The younger you are when you make the switch, the more realistic it is to expect both.

Emotional Risk: A Fallback Plan

Attempting a career change while you are still young enough to bounce back if it doesn't pan out is less risky than having all of your eggs in the proverbial basket later in life. Let's say that you've decided to wait until retirement to try out a new career, with the idea that it will provide you with an ideal amount of supplementary income as well as personal enjoyment. Let's further assume that you've downsized, relocated, or made other major adjustments in your life to accommodate this new career choice, only to discover the dream was nothing like the reality. Furthermore, the reality is awful. If you make this discovery once you've retired, you are more likely to feel a sense of powerlessness. Diminished finances, energy, and professional networks may leave you feeling "trapped" in what you formerly conceived of as your "dream job."

It's far easier to regroup and recover emotionally from a situation such as this before you become heavily invested emotionally and financially. In addition to having a greater chance of being hired in your new career at a younger age, you also have more options for a fallback plan if that new career isn't what you pictured.

Now that you've read a bit about the risks involved in a career change (as well as the risks of waiting!), consider it on a personal level. Answer the following questions in this . . .

REALITY CHECK

- Have I considered the negative aspects to my new career?
- What are the factors preventing me from making a change today? Will they be better or worse in the future?
- Is my age now a better fit as a "rookie" in my chosen career, or will I benefit from waiting?

Your Relationship Could Depend on It

Regardless of your current relationship status, changing careers to do what you love has the potential to impact you in ways you never imagined. Whether you're single, married, or divorced, your choice of career and your level of satisfaction with it will impact your ability to attract the right mate as well as maintain a healthy relationship with your partner.

If You've Never Been Married

Maybe you're just starting out in life and haven't had the time to pursue romantic entanglements. Or maybe you're well into your career and have been so focused on it that nothing else has mattered, until now. The most foolproof way to attract (and keep!) the best lifelong partner for you is to meet someone when you're feeling self-realized and happy. Taking the time to make your career change while you're still single puts you in the enviable position of only having to worry about meeting your own needs. You are free to make the best decisions for you, then meet the right partner when you're no longer seeking happiness from someone else.

If You're Married

If you're like most people, you bring your work home with you. Those of us who love our jobs tend to go on and on about the projects we're currently involved in, while those who hate their work seem to bring a cloud of negativity with them wherever they go.

One surefire relationship killer is to have one party in each circumstance. When this happens, resentment can build as one person's self-esteem withers while their mate seems to flourish. This can happen to virtually anyone, no matter how strong the relationship seems at the outset. Many couples today are faced with aging parents, loss of job security, worries about health care, and increasingly, raising their grandchildren full-time. No matter your age, the pressures we face today are numerous, and when compounded by having to report day in and day out to a job that is no longer fulfilling, it's not surprising when the pressure erupts on the home front.

Contrast this scenario with one where both partners are happy and fulfilled in their respective careers. Rather than coming home in a bad mood, each partner has the ability to make positive emotional contributions to their union. Having a sense of purpose and fulfillment not only improves your own happiness, but your level of attractiveness to your mate as well.

If You're Divorced

The older you are, the greater the chance that you've already been faced with a divorce in your life. It's sad to say, but many adults find it easier to switch spouses than to change careers. Divorce today can be relatively quick, inexpensive, and socially acceptable. Changing careers, on the other hand, can involve a considerable financial investment, going back to school, and redefining yourself in unfamiliar waters. The irony is that sometimes a career change can be instrumental in saving a marriage!

Stop and think about the role career dissatisfaction may have played in your own divorce, and be careful that you don't repeat the same mistake. Statistics show that not only are many second and third marriages failing to thrive, but that divorce rates are actually beginning to rise with age.

Before you make the emotional investment in a new relationship, take the time and energy to invest in your new career. Chances are both you and your future mate will be glad you did!

Now that you've read a bit about how your career choice can impact your relationships, consider it on a personal level. Answer the following questions in this . . .

REALITY CHECK

- Will my partner be supportive of my new career?
- How will my relationship benefit from my new career?
- How might it suffer?
- Have I discussed these scenarios with my mate, and do we feel confident it's the best choice for us as a couple?
- Will my mate also be pursuing a life-altering change? How might this affect my own plans?

Your Health Could Depend on It

In addition to impacting your relationships, your level of career satisfaction (or lack thereof) has the potential to seriously impact your health. In a 2007 study, the *American Journal of Public Health* published a report finding that job stress can be a significant source of depression. That same month, another study linked depression to increased coronary disease. It seems that workplace stress doubles the odds of heart trouble, including heart attacks!

Is your job making you sick? If so, you've probably already considered looking for a new one. Unfortunately, a mere change of venue also carries the risk that you'll be jumping from the proverbial frying pan into the fire. Changing "jobs" might make things worse: changing "careers" is likely a better option. (We'll look at this in detail in Chapter 13.)

Women and Job Stress

For women, job stress can lead to additional issues. Recent studies show that high-stress jobs are significantly associated with earlier menopause among women with no history of depression. Among women with a history of depression, earlier menopause was significantly associated with low job control. You might know women like this—they might be in your office, or related to you—or you might be one of them!

Anne's *Story*

Due to Anne's deep level of dissatisfaction with her job, she found herself depressed. Depression led to weight gain . . . a lot of it. The more weight she gained, the more depressed she became, and the more reluctant she was to expose herself to rejection by applying for other jobs.

At six feet one, Anne was always considered a "large girl," so she was always able to carry a little extra weight on her larger frame. She started eating for comfort, sometimes a tub of ice cream a night, with hot fudge sauce. Before she knew it, she was up to 350 pounds. The wake-up call came when she was visiting a friend in Arizona and wanted to go on a helicopter tour of the Grand Canyon. "They said I was too heavy for the ride," she explains, "and that's when it hit me."

Anne made the decision to investigate gastric bypass. After losing close to forty pounds on her own, she had the surgery, which was largely paid for by the insurance she had through her employer. Today, she feels ready to finally tackle a career change. Not only does she feel better than ever, but her weight loss has given her the self-confidence to go out on the job market and find a better job. ●

Older Workers and Layoffs

In addition to the health risks associated with remaining in a job you don't like, there are the health risks involved in losing that job. The longer you stay in your current job, the greater the chance that you'll one day deal with being laid off. The days of corporate loyalty have long passed. Instead, as we age, we find our jobs threatened by the shifting of employment to overseas markets, increased technology and computerization, and competition from a younger, more skilled work force.

You might be wondering, "Why should I be worried about being laid off? I'll just use that opportunity to embark on my new career choice." One very good reason is that layoffs—even from jobs we hate—are inordinately stressful. Studies show that being laid off in middle age can subtract as much as two years from your life!

In one study, workers who were part of a mass layoff saw their mortality rate worsen over a five-year period and then stay at that higher rate for the next twenty years. All in all, a worker who's been laid off in midlife can expect to live two years less than his luckier counterparts. These statistics alone should inspire you to be an active participant in your career direction, rather than passively waiting for circumstances to force you into a choice.

In short, effecting a career change today is likely not only to improve your mental health, but your overall health and lifespan as well.

Now that you've read a bit about how job stress can impact one's health, consider it on a personal level. Answer the following questions in this . . .

REALITY CHECK

- What is my attitude about my current job?
- Have I been a poor performer because of my attitude?
- Am I depressed?
- Is my health suffering because of my job?
- Do I face increased chances of being let go due to outsourcing overseas or a significant influx of younger workers?

Live for Today, not Tomorrow

Tomorrow may never come—at least not in the form you expect it. If you wait until "one day" to pursue your dreams, you may find yourself facing a radically altered landscape. In addition to having to deal with rapid changes technology, you may have a different partner, different physical abilities, or face different family obligations.

Mark and Donna's *Story*

Mark works as a city employee and Donna is an elementary school teacher. During their twenty-eight years of marriage, they raised two children while working full-time. They had an aggressive savings plan and were planning on retiring at fifty-five. Their dream was to purchase and run a bed-and-breakfast in the Smoky Mountains. Then one day, long after they'd gotten used to their empty nest, their doorbell rang. After escaping an abusive marriage, their daughter found herself on the slippery slope of substance abuse. After ten years on their own, Mark and Donna were suddenly faced with the prospect of raising their daughter's two-year-old son. If they didn't take their grandchild in, Family Services would place him in a foster home. "This is not what I had in mind for fifty," says Donna. Instead of a bed–and–breakfast, the couple recently purchased a time-share and continue to work in their old jobs. "The benefits are good," shares Mark. "That's important when you're raising a two-year-old."

According to the AARP, more than six million children—approximately one in twelve—are living in households headed by grandparents (including grandparents in their forties!). In many of these homes, grandparents and other relatives are taking on primary responsibility for the children's needs. Often, as in the case of Mark and Donna, they assume this responsibility without either of the child's parents present in the home.

For Mark and Donna, this situation means that their dream of running a bed-and-breakfast in the Smoky Mountains will likely never be fulfilled. Had they started sooner, they would have been much better equipped to handle the financial risk and long hours involved in starting a new venture. By the time their grandson came into their lives, the B&B would have been up and running, making it easier to take on this new responsibility and live their dream too. ●

Partners Change

Given the prevailing high rate of divorce, it's not unlikely that you may find yourself with a different partner as you grow older. If you're fortunate enough to have the same partner, your individual goals may have changed. Perhaps your partner has developed a serious health condition, one that prevents you from switching health insurance companies or obtaining new coverage. Or, your partner may have career aspirations of her own that prevent you from making the change simultaneously. Eventually, this could translate to a situation where one risky venture is enough for your marriage and finances, and your own dream may never be realized. Finally, you may find yourself widowed, leaving you without the emotional and financial support you were counting on from your spouse.

Looking at the previous scenarios, it doesn't seem unlikely that something about your present partnership may change, seriously impacting your future ability to live out your dream. There is truly no time like the present!

Technology Changes Everything

Not only might your personal landscape be altered, but it's virtually guaranteed that the entire global picture will have changed by the time you make your move. The main catalyst? Technology.

Technological change is proceeding at an exponential, rather than linear, rate. According to Ray Kurzweil, noted futurist and artificial intelligence expert, because of the fact that we're doubling the rate of technological progress every decade, we'll see a century of progress—at today's rate—in only twenty-five calendar years!

That said, the job you are dreaming of today could be radically altered in some distant "tomorrow," if it even still exists. In the last twenty years, dozens of professions have been left in the proverbial dust by technology. Travel agencies are a prime example: given the abundance of easy-to-use (and free!) travel sites available to the consumer, this profession is now virtually defunct. Similarly affected industries include music, newspapers, and book publishing. The role of librarian has migrated from keeper of the card catalogue to expert in online databases. On a smaller scale, wood and metal workers find it hard to compete with computer-aided manufacturing. Cashiers are increasingly being replaced by automatic checkout stands. Instructors have had to migrate from brick-and-mortar classrooms to virtual learning environments. Sites such as Match.com have largely supplanted traditional matchmaking services. The list goes on. By entering your selected field today, not only do you stand a greater chance of being hired as a younger worker, but you also have a decreased chance of being left behind on the technology curve.

Now that we've discussed the many potential ways our future landscape can be altered, consider it on a personal level. Answer the following questions in this . . .

REALITY CHECK

- What is my role as provider to my family?
- Are there family members who might need my financial support in the future?
- Will I be able to provide it after the career change?
- How might my chosen career be affected by technology?
- Will tomorrow find me better or less equipped than today to adapt to technological changes?

SUMMARY NOW IS THE TIME FOR A CAREER CHANGE BECAUSE:

- Success is not a summit you reach after a lifetime of climbing, but a feeling of satisfaction you can experience daily by doing what you love.
- The younger you are, the less taxing the physical strains involved in a career change will be: going back to school, moving, downsizing, researching, and networking.
- Most people underestimate the costs of a career change while overestimating their retirement income. Do what you can today to reduce the cost side of the equation.
- Risky ventures are more advisable in your younger years, when you are more likely to bounce back, both emotionally and financially.
- Your marriage is likely to benefit from a happier you. Having a sense of purpose and fulfillment not only improves your own happiness but your level of attractiveness to your mate.
- Embarking on a satisfying career change now may avoid a full-on "midlife crisis" later.
- Remaining in a high-stress job can lead to depression, weight gain, and heart problems: carefully weigh the material gains of staying in your current job against the health strains.
- Your employer might offer benefits today that you won't have access to tomorrow. Take advantage of them so you can start your new life in the best shape ever!
- Tomorrow may be vastly different from today: emotionally, physically, economically, and technologically. Seize the opportunity that exists today!

CHAPTER 2

How Will This Change My Life?

Change is the one thing that all living creatures fear above all else. The irony is that personal growth can only occur when we step outside of our comfort zones, either for good or for ill. Unfortunately, it's called a "comfort zone" for a reason: it's often easier to remain lulled into a sense of complacency (even while we're in a job we dislike!) than it is to take the first step onto an unknown path, hoping it will lead to a better life.

To make taking that first step easier, it helps to clearly outline how your life will improve, how it might suffer, and which factors are unknowable until after you take the plunge—and whether or not you can handle the uncertainty.

The Plusses

Thanks to the success of books such as *The 4-Hour Workweek*, a lot of working-age adults are actively seeking "lifestyle careers." These are careers that allow individuals the freedom to focus on the things that matter most (relationships, quality of life, giving to others) instead of basing their success on annual salaries or net worth. Pick up any newspaper or national magazine these days and you're likely to find at least one success story of someone who has stepped off the fast track and onto the path of their dreams. Oftentimes, these individuals go on to launch very successful businesses, or start nonprofits that touch a lot of lives. (We'll meet quite a few of these individuals in Part 3.)

Finding Your Perfect Match

There are two approaches to embarking on this type of career change. The first, more conventional way, is to apply for a job in your new field that is a better match for your temperament, relationships, and interests.

As the following story shows, sometimes the toughest challenge is identifying *your own priorities*, rather than simply following society's proscription.

Nanette's *Story*

Nanette was on the fast track to success. In college, she focused her attention on finishing as quickly as possible, while maintaining a perfect GPA. Thanks to her hard work and dedication, she managed to obtain a job as the manager of a midsize department for a major D.C. lobbyist group. She had a good salary, great benefits, and a high level of visibility. By the time she hit thirty, she'd spearheaded a well-cited industry white paper and had appeared before senior government officials to present her work.

On the personal side of equation, things were a mess. Thanks to her drive and ambition, her marriage fell apart and her health started to deteriorate. Just like in college, there simply wasn't any room in her life for fun or relaxation.

After several years of searching, Nanette alleviated some of this self-imposed pressure to fit in by moving to a smaller town and taking a job managing the town library. It took her out of the fast-paced setting she'd been operating in but allowed her a little bit of prestige by remaining in management. The demands of the library were nowhere near the pressure of her old job. The commute was also short and free of traffic, which meant that she still arrived home in time to enjoy quality time with her new husband, as well as fit in some time for herself. Since her job didn't carry the emotional pressure of needing to "get ahead," she had more energy on the weekends to spend time outdoors or with friends.

Ironically, Nanette would never have appreciated this type of job straight out of college. Instead, it took first achieving a more traditional form of success for her to realize that personal relationships mattered more to her than the amount of her take-home pay. ●

Creating Your Own Perfect Match

The second approach is to become what is known as a "lifestyle entrepreneur," or to go into business for yourself and doing the very thing you love. This approach allows greater freedom and flexibility when it comes to setting hours, choosing projects, and living where you want. The next story clearly illustrates the benefits of this approach.

Clive's *Story*

By the age of thirty-three, Clive was living what society would judge a fairly "successful" life. The software marketing executive had a cushy job, a six-figure income with lots of perks, the opportunity to travel all over Europe on an expense account, and a company car. You might be wondering, "What more could someone like that want?"

The truth is, Clive was under so much stress that his job was slowly killing him. By his own admission, he smoked and drank too much and seemed to always feel angry. After taking an extensive sabbatical, Clive emerged with a new understanding of what he truly wanted in his life —and it wasn't a six-figure income or a company car.

Today, Clive works as a personal lifestyle coach, helping others venture into more fulfilling careers and lifestyle choices. He and his wife (also a coach) live in a beautiful house in the San Juan Islands, working just two to three days per week. This is partially possible because Clive and his family have balanced their material needs against their spiritual, emotional, and physical needs. The rest of their time is spent enjoying all that the beautiful Pacific Northwest has to offer and spending quality time with their baby daughter, Iona. ●

The Minuses

No career choice on the planet is without its downsides. Believing otherwise is to set yourself up for disappointment right from the start. The key is to clearly identify the negative aspects of your new career ahead of time and understanding that there are differences between short-term and long-term scenarios.

Understanding Your Limitations

For example, let's examine the "lifestyle entrepreneur" path. It's important to realize that this approach carries with it considerably greater risk and usually involves a significant investment of time to get your business up and running. Many career changers embark on this path with rose-colored glasses firmly in place. Looking at Clive's example, he didn't go from an eighty-hour work week to working two to three days a week overnight. He had to obtain his training and certifications as a coach and build his client base (no easy task) while moving across an ocean. However, Clive didn't go into his new path blind to the initial sacrifices, unlike James.

James's *Story*

James was working as a graphic artist for a midsize marketing firm. He enjoyed the artistic aspects of his job but did not enjoy the layers of bureaucracy between his work and the final end user. He longed to open his own graphic design studio and escape the confines of his cubicle.

Fast-forward to several years into the future. James was able to locate clients and produce the kind of material that wasn't possible in a staid corporate setting. But there was a problem: James was no businessman. All too often, he found himself waiting for months on end to be paid for completed work. He also had to deal with clients who expected revisions to their websites to go on infinitum (for no additional charge), and many times found himself with other problems caused by poorly communicated intentions. Worst of all, James never got into the habit of using written contracts for his projects, and on more than one occasion had to walk away from a project without payment nor suitable recourse. As much as James hated his corporate job, he hadn't appreciated the vital role the company played in negotiating contracts and ensuring a steady income stream.

Due to the fact that he was perpetually late getting paid, he was constantly seeking more work. Eventually, he found that the number of hours he was work-ing had increased to sixteen to eighteen hours per day. He ended up feeling more stressed being self-employed than he'd been uncomfortable in the cubicle.

Having renounced the corporate lifestyle, he struggled for years with the deci-sion to return to a full-time job, working for someone else. Today, he is employed in another setting he doesn't enjoy but is planning a move back into entrepreneur-ship. This time, he is going to do it right: partnering with a business-minded person to handle sales, negotiations, and payment, and making sure that every part of his plan is documented by written contracts. ●

In addition to the career-specific changes (i.e., having to take on a more business-oriented role, expanding your creative side, salary changes, etc.) there will also be several external factors involved in your career change—both tangible and intangible—as we'll see next.

Changing Location or Downsizing

Making your change may or may not involve a change in location. Even if you stay in the same town, downsizing your home may be in order.

There are three main reasons you may consider downsizing now rather than later.

Smoother Sailing Later

According to professional organizer Sunny Schlenger (a successful career-changer we'll get to know in Chapter 15), "It's much easier emotionally if you're proactive." Sunny shares, "Since I love organizing, I'd always organize and rearrange my parents' possessions whenever I visited them throughout the years." When they passed away, she and her brother were able to quickly sort through the estate within two days, without the added emotional burden of sorting through mountains of personal items. When it comes to job-changers, the same thing applies. What if you don't believe that a job change will require a move, but you eventually find yourself having to relocate after all? If you've already eliminated the bulk of what you don't want, you'll be in a much freer state to pick up the pieces and move on to your new destination.

Free Up Some Cash

The second reason is financial. As I wrote in *Unplugged*, most of us are surrounded by "sprinkles." Using the analogy of a cake: the cake itself has flavor and so does the frosting. But what do the sprinkles really add? Empty calories. Take a good look around you. Chances are, you're surrounded by things that you no longer use and likely never will. At some point in this process, you should definitely consider eliminating the sprinkles. (We'll talk about this more in Chapter 4, when we'll discuss how to convert clutter into cash to help pad your transition time.)

Free Up Your Time

The third reason is that, as Sunny puts it, "Belongings require maintenance." Whether it's cleaning them, sorting them, keeping track of them, or the mere fact that they take up real estate in your house, you expend energy on your possessions. Simplifying your possessions allows you to redirect that energy into your new career—and you'll need it!

If your plan includes a complete change of venue, be sure you apply the tips in Chapter 8 ("Stick Your Big Toe In: The Trial Run") to ensure you have realistic expectations of your new home base. In addition to climate, cost of living, and other issues discussed in that chapter, there are also several intangibles you'll need to consider.

You Can't Touch This: The Importance of Intangibles

Life is made of intangibles: our job duties, salaries, and living arrangements are all building blocks, but intangibles are the glue that binds them together into a happy life. You can have a solid career and comfortable home, but if your friends, social network, and local culture are unsatisfactory, you will soon grow unhappy in your new circumstances.

The two keys to success when it comes to dealing with these intangible elements are flexibility and tolerance.

Bend, Don't Break: Flexibility

Ask any experienced world traveler what the key to a successful trip is, and you'll likely hear: "flexibility!" Frank, who has been to over 100 countries, agrees. If you have the time, this septuagenarian will tell you all about the time that he went to Egypt on a three-week cruise, only to find that upon arriving at the airport in Cairo, his luggage hadn't made it. Since his ship left the next day, he had a limited amount of time to purchase some ill-fitting clothes before departing for his journey. Thanks to his height (six feet two), Frank had a difficult time finding clothes in the Egyptian markets that fit him. Those who know him well couldn't believe that this conservative gentleman had to resort to wearing a djellaba for part of the time and laundering his underwear nightly until his luggage finally caught up to him, halfway through the trip.

Did this misadventure stop Frank from traveling? Did he decide not to go on the cruise, for fear of what other people would think of his strange outfit? No! In fact, he's added several dozen countries since that time, but now knows enough to pack at least one change of clothes and additional underwear in his carry-on luggage.

You might be wondering why Frank's story is relevant. In truth, what is Life but the biggest journey of all? Savvy career-changers need to think like savvy travelers: you need to understand that despite the best-thought-out itineraries, your luggage (or more appropriately, your "baggage"!) may not survive the journey. Can you be flexible? Can you adapt to changing circumstances by focusing on the good parts of your adventure while putting the mishaps in perspective? Or are you the type of traveler who would be so upset at having to cruise for three weeks with no luggage that you'd cancel the trip, missing out on a once-in-a-lifetime adventure?

Avoid Being Judge and Jury: Tolerance

The other keystone to a successful journey is tolerance. Just as you wouldn't go on a tour of the Vatican wearing nothing but a swimsuit, you shouldn't presume to waltz into your new career, town, and social circle expecting to bring your existing mindset and social norms with you intact.

If you move to a smaller town, can you leave the pushiness and "survival of the fittest" big-city mentality behind? Can you refrain from judging those with a slower pace of life and slower speech patterns? It's amazing how many people move to small towns after reading about them in magazine articles such as "The Fifty Best Places to Live," and then expect to find everything they left behind. "Where's the Starbucks? Where's the Trader Joe's?" they wonder. "Why don't these people drive faster? Why do they want to talk about the weather before giving me my change at the grocery store?"

If you're moving to a larger town for your change, the opposite is true. Can you deal with the loss of warmth and familiarity involved with big-city life? Are you able to refrain from taking things personally?

Most importantly, can you adapt to new mindsets while still being yourself? Anyone can pretend to be tolerant, but be warned that your true colors will eventually show through. To be able to make and enjoy real connections and friendships, you will need an open mind and an open heart.

Dealing with the Unknown

Hopefully by now you realize the importance of doing your research, a topic further expanded upon in Chapters 7 and 8. But no matter how well you think you've prepared for your career change, something unforeseen is bound to happen. Why do I say this? Because like snowflakes, no two individuals are truly alike. Whether you decide to move to the San Juan Islands and operate a coaching business, or start your own graphics design firm, you will face a completely different set of challenges, opportunities, and decisions than those faced by Clive or James.

So, you have to ask yourself: "How comfortable am I dealing with the unexpected?" Of course, by the time you work through the steps in this book, you'll have a vision and solid plan, which should be a source of immense comfort as you face the inevitable bumps in the road. The advice contained herein has been carefully constructed to minimize your obstacles and setbacks, but again, no plan is foolproof. We'll be looking in detail at strategies for dealing with the unknown in the next chapter.

Now, let's examine the concepts we've looked at in this chapter to see if right now, you feel a career change is truly "worth it" to you. You may find it helpful to write down your thoughts in a notebook or to discuss these issues with your friends or family. As you answer each question, try to think of specific instances to support your opinion.

Checklist | Is It Worth It?

How many of these statements do you agree with?

○ I have a good grasp of my own strengths and weaknesses, and my new career will strongly favor my strengths.

○ I am willing to be flexible and understand that "life has a way of happening while you're making plans." I feel confident that even if things don't go 100 percent according to plan (as they almost surely will not), I will seek to find new ways to adapt to my changing circumstances, neither giving up nor stubbornly refusing to accept reality.

○ I am willing to practice tolerance. I am capable of reserving judgment regarding new ideas, philosophies, religions, and cultures as I interact with my new neighbors, peers, and clients. I will not try to impose my belief system and worldview onto my new setting.

○ I understand that while having solid building blocks (the right job, home, partner) is important, happiness is constructed from the intangible glue that binds these blocks together.

If there are any items you don't agree with, now is the time to evaluate the reasons and deal with any issues that could be holding you back.

SUMMARY YOU'RE READY TO CHANGE YOUR LIFE BECAUSE:

- Fulfillment matters more to you than artificially defined "success."
- You want to focus on your own values rather than on a corporation's bottom line.
- The plusses outweigh the minuses, and you feel fairly comfortable knowing what they are.
- You are generally tolerant of new ideas, philosophies, people, and cultures—all of which you are bound to encounter in your new setting.
- Like a good traveler, you understand the importance of flexibility.

CHAPTER 3

Am I Ready Emotionally?

As you embark on your career change, many factors are likely to change. These include, but are not limited to, your income, lifestyle, friends, location, health benefits, and your future outlook. Obviously, when we consider a career change, we expect most of these changes to be favorable. Many times, however, the negative changes will be felt while you're in transition from your old job to your new job. Thus, it's crucial to have the appropriate emotional mechanisms in place.

Drastic Changes Can Have Drastic Consequences

It's likely that your career change will include at least one or two of the six factors listed on page 29. The fewer the changes, and the slower the pace at which you must adapt to them, the easier your transition will be. For example, if your new career involves a pay cut, but not a change in location, you'll find comfort in the familiarity of your surroundings and the proximity of your family and friends. Some career changes, however, can involve such drastic lifestyle adjustments that they can seriously impact your self-worth and mental well-being.

What can you do to prevent having a career-change meltdown? There are three keys: a solid support network, the help of a coach or mentor, and an accountability system. Using one or a combination of these keys will go a long way toward providing you the emotional support necessary for your job change.

Your Support Network

If you are the type that can take unexpected challenges in stride, good for you! However, even the best spirited among us have down days. Should you happen to hit a roadblock on a day you're feeling down, it's important that you have a good support network standing by to lift you up and push you forward.

Your support network needn't be large. But it's vital that the members live up to the "support" part of the phrase. Anyone who questions your career change (especially once you've addressed their concerns) should not be included. I don't mean that you should excommunicate these people completely, just that they should not be part of the inner circle you turn to for advice or when the chips are down.

There is a certain kind of personality type out there (I call them "vampires") that feed on other people's misery and failure. Unfortunately, they tend to be just the type of person most people invite into their inner circles. Good listeners, vampires position themselves as the compassionate friend you can turn to for solid advice. But there is a reason this type of person makes a great confidant: they love to listen to your problems! "Well, so does a good friend, a non-vampire," you might say. "How do I tell them apart?" Vampires also follow another pattern. When you encounter a roadblock on the path to success (especially if this success involves change), the vampire will often adopt an I-told-you-so attitude and encourage you to drop your endeavor altogether. On the flip side, they also manage to taint your successes. Often, this is subtly done: you walk away from the encounter wondering why you suddenly feel down after sharing good news.

The truth is that some people are so afraid of change that they are resentful of those who have the courage and fortitude to take a chance at making their own dreams come true. As you embark on your journey, it's vital that you understand and recognize who your allies are and whom you should exclude from your inner circle.

Consider Hiring a Coach

If, on the other hand, you're the type who is easily thrown off kilter by unexpected challenges, you'll not only need a solid support network, but you may also consider the services of a coach. Your coach can help keep your problems in perspective and also keep you centered on your goal.

There are a lot of people out there calling themselves "coaches." What exactly is a coach, anyway? As coach Clive Prout explains it, "A mentor is someone who uses their life experiences to guide you. A coach is a paid professional trained to help you reach new levels of growth, drawing from your own personal and professional experiences." A mentor often takes a more one-size-fits-all approach; a coach sees the beauty in the snowflake.

What to Look for in a Coach

If you do decide to hire a coach, check out her credentials and ask for references. Also make sure that this is someone you like and trust enough to establish a good rapport. You'll accomplish nothing if you hire someone with whom you don't feel comfortable sharing your innermost doubts and worries.

Subject Matter Expertise

First, the person you choose should be a subject matter expert in his field. The field, in turn, should be very closely related to what you're trying to achieve. For example, if you're contemplating a career change, you'd want someone who is an expert in career changes, not just in "life goals." The more specific, the better. Sunny Schlenger is an organizational coach, but she won't help you whip your closets into shape. Rather, her specialty is getting your life organized for maximum efficiency.

Background in Counseling

Second, the coach should have some type of background in counseling. Sunny, who has a master's in psychology, has found herself in situations where a client's life was spiraling so out of control, so fast, that she had to "talk him down" from the ledge of a disastrous outcome. Not all coaches have academic backgrounds in psychology. However, if they have been certified by a reputable organization, such as the Coaches Training Institute, then they have received the appropriate training.

Shared Values

Third, your coach should understand, and be in agreement with, your ultimate goal. Some coaches—especially those newer to the profession—may take on any client, regardless of their own beliefs. For obvious reasons, this type of coaching will not be very effective in the long run. Hiring a coach can be expensive, but so is making it almost to the finish line and changing your mind in the face of an obstacle. Your coach's fee will pay for itself at moments like those, because you can turn to him for unbiased advice that is bound to get you back on track.

Make Yourself Accountable

It's a measurable fact that those who attempt to do things alone (stop smoking, lose weight, go back to school) are not as effective as those who have a partner. If hiring a coach is out of the question financially, at the very minimum you should seek out an accountability partner. This person should be someone who is also in the process of a career change. It need not be your spouse or romantic partner—in fact, it's preferable if this person is not your mate. (After all, sometimes your obstacle on the path to success is your mate or a close family member!)

There are many ways to locate an accountability partner. Social networking sites are ideal for this, because you don't necessarily have to meet in person. That said, regularly scheduled, in-the-flesh meetings are the most effective because they are harder to blow off. Other options for locating a partner include sites such as MeetUp.com, your local community college or university, or local networking groups specific to your new career.

To ensure your meetings don't devolve into a coffee klatch, you should design a preprinted card with specific questions that you each have to address at each meeting. A business-size card is best, so that you can tuck it into your wallet. It's a good idea to have it laminated, as well.

Questions for the card could include:

- What have I done this week to further my goal?
- How is my family/significant other dealing with the change?
- What other emotional obstacles am I facing this week?
- What are my financial issues this week?
- How am I doing in terms of health and fitness this week?

It's important to keep the discussions focused on this week (or month if you only meet monthly). For one thing, it prevents the problems from taking on a larger than life aspect.

Use the card to go through the questions one at a time, and take turns answering them. A productive meeting need only take an hour for two participants, longer for more. Having three people has the potential to work better than just two people, since it improves the chances that at least one of your accountability partners will be at the meeting. A group of four people is usually too large to effectively move through the questions, although it can work with a forceful moderator. With fewer participants there is a greater chance of moving through the card and dealing with each member's issues.

A word of caution: When choosing an accountability partner, choose someone who has zero chance of becoming a romantic partner. If you are a heterosexual woman, choose a woman, not a man. As you move through this life-changing process, you'll be dealing with many intense feelings. The last thing you want to happen is to jeopardize your current relationship by misplacing those feelings in favor of your accountability partner. If this happens (on either side) objectivity will be lost and problems are sure to follow.

Now, let's examine the concepts we've looked at in this chapter to see if right now, you feel a career change is truly "worth it" to you. You may find it helpful to write down your thoughts in a notebook or to discuss these issues with your friends or family. As you answer each question, try to think of specific instances to support your opinion.

Checklist | Is It Worth It?
How many of these statements do you agree with?

○ I understand that no career path on earth is perfect: there's a downside to everything. However, the downside of remaining in my current job is much greater than the anticipated downside of my new career.

○ I am aware that all change, even for the better, involves risk and some degree of stress. I have (or will have) the mechanisms in place to cope when the going gets tough, such as a coach or support network.

○ I have a good grasp of my own strengths and weaknesses, and my new career will strongly favor my strengths.

○ I am willing to make short-term significant sacrifices of time, resources, and emotional energy to achieve a long-term future that is more in line with my core values.

If there are any items you don't agree with, now is the time to evaluate the reasons and deal with any issues that could be holding you back.

SUMMARY YOU'RE READY TO CHANGE YOUR LIFE BECAUSE:

- Unexpected bumps in the road aren't enough to deter you from achieving your dream.
- You have a strong support network to keep you centered.
- You have enlisted the services of a coach or an accountability partner to keep you on track.

CHAPTER 4

Am I Ready Financially?

You've probably heard the adage, "If you fail to plan, you plan to fail." Never is this more true than when applied to your financial decisions. The wrong financial decision or an unexpected expense can ultimately affect your mental, emotional, and even physical well-being, not to mention derail your career change completely. That said, it's vital that you take a close look at your current, transitional, and future finances.

Meeting Current Obligations

During your transition phase, you'll need to meet both your existing obligations as well as increased expenses for training, certifications, travel to investigate opportunities and locations, and more.

Establishing a Baseline

The first step is to record your current expenses in order to establish a valid baseline. There are two main approaches to this: keeping an expense journal for thirty days in which you record every single expense, or creating a paper trail by consistently using your debit card for everything. (Note: debit, not credit!) Most people are shocked when they sit down and look at what they are actually spending money on (or what their mate is spending money on). The first step is to trade in your rose-colored glasses for some reading glasses, and get real.

Cutting the Fat

Once you've identified what you're actually spending money on, the next step is to identify what you need to stop spending money on: Where can you cut the fat? Are you drinking $5 or more per day in fancy lattes? Do you buy lunch every day? Rather than watching your money go down the drain, try to find ways to reduce these types of consumption as much as possible. While your goal is not an ascetic lifestyle, you do need to be conscious that every dollar squandered puts you several paces behind on the road to success.

Sticking to a Budget

Once you've written down your minimum monthly obligations and the items you'd like to eliminate, create a budget. There are several factors to keep in mind when creating a budget. First, it needs to be in writing. Whether you use a simple Excel spreadsheet, fancy budgeting software, or a plain spiral notebook, make sure you put it in black and white. Second, get everyone's commitment. If you are the only one sticking to the budget while your partner and/or dependents keep spending like there's no tomorrow, you've accomplished nothing. Third, build in some fun. While you do want to scale back somewhat on luxuries, be sure you plan for entertainment (dinners out, movies, hobbies, travel, etc.). This will go a long way toward gaining the cooperation of your spouse and family, as well as ensuring you're not tempted to cheat. Fourth, try to use cash for miscellaneous and entertainment expenses. While it's true that we are converting to a cashless society, using cash has several advantages. First, it's easier to understand that buying that gizmo or gadget may mean not eating lunch out on Saturday with your friends. Second, it's been proven that people who use cash are less apt to make impulse purchases.

When creating your budget, the goal is to live below your means for a while. Remember, in addition to your current obligations, you'll need to create space for those transitional expenses. You also need to shore up your savings. There is likely to come a day when you'll need a buffer, especially if you're going into business for yourself.

Reducing Debt

At this point in your life, it's very likely that you are far from being debt-free (If you are, double kudos. You may proceed to the next section.) Most Baby Boomers, however, are apt to find themselves in a worse position today than they were ten or even twenty years ago, thanks to the double burden of caring for elderly parents and providing financial support for their children and grandchildren. Sixty-six percent of Baby Boomers surveyed by the International Association of Financial Planning said "providing long-term care for a parent would affect their ability to save for their children's education" and would no doubt also affect their ability to save for their own retirement. Rising medical costs are also taking their toll.

But it's not just members of this generation who are in trouble. Both Boomers and Gen-Xers have completely bought into the materialist view of self-worth, although they spend their money on different things. Boomers have traditionally gone for the big houses and fancy cars, while younger generations are increasingly preoccupied with fancy technological gadgets. In addition to mounting debt, both generations are saving significantly less than their parents and grandparents, largely due to a reliance on easy credit.

There are three main factors you need to consider when looking at reducing your debt: your house, your car, and your credit cards. Let's look at each of these separately, as well as review some important tips on the pitfalls and perils of debt restructuring in general.

Your House

Let's start by looking at what is likely your biggest expense: your home. If you're still making mortgage payments, it's in your best interests to investigate refinancing your home at a lower rate. Refinancing is usually not worth it unless you can get a rate that is at least 2 percentage points lower than your current rate. Otherwise, between origination and other fees, you may end up spending more than what you'll save on the lower payments.

Another tactic is to request the removal of PMI (private mortgage insurance) from your payments. If you've had your mortgage for more than two years and your loan balance is now less than 80 percent of your home's value, you should request your lender to remove PMI. If you've been making timely payments, this shouldn't be a problem. Otherwise, you may wish to refinance and ask for no PMI at that time. This could potentially save you hundreds of dollars per month. All you have to do to find out if this is possible is to have your home appraised and compare the appraised value to what you owe.

In addition to refinancing at a lower rate, you may also consider switching to a biweekly mortgage plan. These plans can drastically reduce the amount of interest you pay while significantly reducing the amount of time it takes to pay off your mortgage. This may be a good option for those of you planning on staying in your current home. Naturally these plans only apply under the assumption that you won't be downsizing to a smaller house as discussed in Chapter 2.

Your Car

The next most significant expense is likely to be your car payment. Here is where you have to make a decision about status versus practicality. If you've recently purchased a new car, a wise strategy might be to sell the new car and purchase a slightly used model instead. Cars lose 20 percent of their value just by driving off the lot, and 65 percent within their first five years.

Your Credit Cards

Most people have at least one credit card that they rely on. The key is to identify if you're relying on your credit cards as income (i.e., to meet your obligations) or if you are in a position to be able to pay them down (and ultimately pay them off completely).

The best strategy for paying off your credit cards is to create a simple debt matrix. This will require about twenty minutes to do, but the payback is enormous. First, identify all of your creditors. Next, find out what the interest rates are that they each charge. Third, organize your list of creditors in order of interest rate, with the highest rate creditor first. Typically, your list will have store credit cards at the very top, and your home mortgage at the bottom. Fourth, write out the monthly payments and how much you owe for each creditor. Your matrix should therefore have four columns: Creditor, Interest Rate, Monthly Payment, and Total Owed.

Here is where some well-intentioned people go astray. While most people understand that it's important to make more than the minimum monthly payment each month (unless you want to be in credit card bondage forever), they usually pay all of their creditors more than the minimum amount. A better, more effective strategy is to tackle these cards one at a time. For example, you should pay the minimum on all of your other monthly bills (or just a little more if it makes you feel better) but pay the maximum you can comfortably afford each month on the highest interest card you have. Once you have paid off the highest card, move on to the next lower one, and so on. Using this strategy will help you make dramatic inroads in reducing your debt.

Finally, you should consider getting rid of as many credit cards as possible. Cut them up, and then write to the credit card company asking them to close your account. Request that they make a note that the account was closed per the request of the cardholder. It's important to wean yourself from the habit of using credit cards. Once you achieve the debt reduction/debt liberation you've worked so hard to get, do everything you can to prevent falling into the same trap.

Problems with Debt Restructuring

There are several pitfalls to debt restructuring that you want to be sure to avoid. Many people use their home equity loans to repay their credit card debt. When you engage in this practice is you are converting your unsecured loan into a secured loan, and that security is your home. Think twice before putting your home at risk. For many people, it's your most valued investment. Don't put yourself in a position where you'll owe money when you do sell.

We've all received the offers in the mail: "0 percent interest!" or "Low rates on balance transfers!" If you do decide to take advantage of these types of offers, be sure you read the fine print. Many credit card companies promise 0 percent interest for one year or until the balance is paid off, but there are often important caveats. The first one is to never be late. Never. Even if you are one day late, you can expect your interest rate to escalate dramatically. The best way to handle balance transfers is to transfer your higher rate balances to a lower card, and then automate your monthly payments. (Feel free to pay the minimum payment as you concentrate on first paying off those higher rate cards. If you have no other cards, then you should make your payments as high as you can comfortably manage. The key is consistency.) A word of warning: Many times these introductory balance transfers will have such a short billing cycle that you will miss your first payment if you're not paying attention. So, be vigilant, read the fine print, and be on time!

The other technique you need to approach with caution is the use of credit consolidation services. While these agencies can help you by negotiating a debt management plan with your creditors, keep the following factors in mind. First, although these services will negotiate lower interest rates and consolidate your bills into one monthly payment, you will also be paying a monthly fee for this service. Since the fees are often based on the number of accounts you need to manage, this can get expensive. Second, you should know that the use of such services can show up as late or reduced payments on your credit report, even if you pay on time. Third, there are many disreputable agencies out there doing business under this umbrella (some of the worst claiming to be "Christian" services). Be sure you fully vet any agency you are considering doing business with; they should be licensed by your state. The last thing you want to do is set up payments to an organization that never forwards them on to your creditors!

Accurately Predicting New Expenses

Once you have a clear understanding of your current obligations and debt ratio, you need to be able to paint a reasonable, accurate portrait of your financial future. There are several ways to get a handle on your future expenses.

Learn What's Deductible

One tip is to ask your accountant for a list of authorized tax deductions for your profession. Chances are you'll see things on that list that you didn't realize you'd be spending money on in the first place, let alone deducting from your taxes.

Join an Association

The second method is to visit the association or professional organization for your profession. These associations often maintain websites with free information, but sometimes membership is required to access them. As we'll see in Part 2, joining a professional association is useful on many levels, so the membership fee is often well worth the money. If you can find a way to fund your membership in a related association by eliminating some of your typical wasteful spending, you won't even feel the pinch.

Obtain Some Personal Perspective

The third method is to confer with someone already in your new profession. Perhaps this person will be the same person you choose for your "ride-along" (see Chapter 8). Feel free to ask them, "What unexpected expenses did you discover your first year in this job?" If you don't ask, no one may ever think to volunteer this information to you.

Converting Clutter into Cash

As we discussed briefly in Chapter 2, eliminating the clutter in your life can provide you with a sizeable chunk of cash you can use to pay for training, education, travel, or other expenses associated with your career change. You can also choose to kick-start your savings for a rainy day with the proceeds. There are three main online markets for your clutter: non-auction reseller auctions, online auction markets, and free classified listings.

Non-Auction Marketplaces

Both Amazon.com and Barnes and Noble's reseller marketplaces are a great place to sell your unwanted books, movies, and music. Since it's not set up as an auction, many users appreciate the straightforward nature of this service. For example, Amazon calculates postage and shipping, and payments are made directly to your checking account. (Buyers simply pay Amazon using whichever form of payment they prefer.) While Amazon does charge a commission, the site makes it easy to determine the worth of your item and to see how many are being sold by other sellers. You can thus set your price accordingly.

Online Auctions

Other items such as clothes, electronics, and collector's items can easily be sold on eBay. Millions of people have bought or sold items on eBay; some have even converted selling other people's junk into a full-time job! Getting started with eBay is relatively simple. If you feel intimidated, chances are pretty good that you have someone in your immediate family who is well versed in it. While there are services out there that will sell your items for you, the service fee they charge can make a significant dent in your earnings. If you do decide to get involved as an active eBay seller, be sure to stay alert for phishing scams. On the eBay website there are often articles and warnings about what to look out for: usually buyers offering to buy your item outside of the auction.

Free Classified Listings

Finally, you can use free classified listings, such as craigslist. This service has several advantages over both Amazon and eBay, the first being that it's free. The second is that it's local, so you don't have to worry about packaging and shipping your item. This service is ideal for larger items (furniture, heavy items) as well as items that are relatively low-cost (and not worth paying a commission to sell). As with eBay, however, scammers often target this service, so exercise caution. Craigslist also posts warnings and tips on their site; be sure to read them.

Grants and Scholarships for Career Changers

Before you decide to take out a loan to finance training for your career change, it's worth the time and effort to research any applicable grants and scholarships that might be available to you. If you're pursuing a career in medicine, education, or the arts, you might be surprised at the variety of opportunities. There are several resources to find this information. I personally recommend books by Matthew Lesko. He has made researching "free money" his life and has an entire series of books devoted to this very topic.

Now, let's examine the concepts we've looked at in this chapter to see if right now, you feel a career change is truly "worth it" to you. You may find it helpful to write down your thoughts in a notebook or to discuss these issues with your friends or family. As you answer each question, try to think of specific instances to support your opinion.

Checklist | Is It Worth It?

How many of these statements do you agree with?

○ I am willing to invest a significant amount of time on understanding and improving my financial picture.

○ I am prepared to scale back on my discretionary spending in the short run to more quickly and comfortably achieve my career change.

○ I am not attached to my possessions or seduced by the thought of obtaining new ones.

○ I can see the importance of downsizing and eliminating debt when making a career change.

○ I am able to practice restraint and consistency to reach my goal.

○ I understand that my expenses may actually rise during my transition between careers.

If there are any statements you don't agree with, now is the time to carefully analyze the reasons why and determine how much of a roadblock this item represents in your overall plan.

SUMMARY I AM FINANCIALLY PREPARED TO MAKE A CHANGE BECAUSE:

- Failing to plan is planning to fail.
- A bad financial decision can negatively affect my health, as well as my mental and emotional well-being.
- I have a good grasp of my debts and assets.
- I have a plan to reduce my debts.

CHAPTER 5

Am I Ready Physically?

By now it's probably obvious that embarking on a career change requires a lot of energy: not just of the emotional variety, but physical energy as well. Until you're ready to take the plunge, you'll be engaging in planning sessions, conducting online and in-person research, and possibly taking classes, all while holding down your current job. Needless to say, maximizing your physical condition will go a long way towards ensuring you have sufficient energy to see the process through.

Will You Need to Get in Shape?

The most common New Year's resolutions are to lose weight, stop smoking, and to get a better job. Why wait until a new calendar year to launch the new you? Take the excitement and momentum generated by your decision to make a career change and use it to transform not just your career, but yourself as a person.

Personal Reasons

There are four good reasons to get in shape before your career change. First, as mentioned above, career changes require a great deal of energy. Second, your new career may be more active in and of itself. Third, being in good physical condition often translates to lower health insurance rates, and if you'll be purchasing private insurance, this can be a significant factor to consider. Finally, getting in shape will likely boost your self-confidence, which will benefit you whether you are applying for a job with a company or seeking new clients for your own business.

Employer Perceptions

Unfortunately, there is also the issue of weight discrimination. Studies by Wayne State and Cornell universities reveal that "the bias appears to be most prominent during the hiring process, when an employer knows a potential employee the least and therefore is most likely to be influenced by stereotypes (such as fat people are lazy)." These studies also show that while being overweight affects both genders and races, overweight white women are evaluated more harshly than their African-American counterparts.

Not only are employers concerned about your personal attributes (laziness vs. a strong work ethic), but they are also concerned about rising health care costs. An article in Forbes, "Is Your Weight Affecting Your Career?" cites a study that shows obese employees cost U.S. private companies an estimated $45 billion annually in medical expenditures and work loss. In addition, other studies show that obese workers file twice the number of workers' compensation claims, have seven times the medical costs, and lose thirteen times the days of work from work injury or illness compared with other employees.

As a result of all of this, it's not surprising that overweight workers find themselves passing phone interviews with flying colors, only to find things deteriorating quickly once they have their first in-person interview. It's not uncommon for your meeting to be cut short or to be abruptly told the position has been filled.

Taking Advantage of Today's Benefits

Anne is a classic example of this strategy. She took advantage of her current company's health insurance to have gastric bypass surgery and went from 350 pounds to 185 pounds, and as a result she gained a tremendous amount of self-confidence in the process. While she still sometimes thinks of herself as "the same old fat person" (which is normal for those going through this process), she has transformed from someone who used to hide behind her weight to someone who is willing to put herself out there, including to potential new employers. One day soon, she hopes to be able to leave the job she hates and move into a more fulfilling career—which wouldn't have been possible without the surgery.

In addition to health insurance coverage for this type of radical surgery, many companies also offer discounted programs (i.e., smoking cessation, gym memberships) designed to inspire healthy lifestyles in their employees. Others offer better overall benefits to those who do their part. ClearChannel Communications is one such company. It offers employees two health plans, one with a relatively high deductible, and one with no deductible (but a higher monthly cost). To qualify for the latter plan, employees must provide evidence of engaging in various "healthy lifestyle" activities throughout the year. These include losing weight, participating in smoking cessation programs, and simple things like getting flu shots. The company also has an online database where employees can log daily exercise and eating habits.

Companies realize that healthy workers are more productive workers, and they cost a lot less to insure. If you need to lose weight, stop smoking, or get counseling for other unhealthy habits, take full advantage of your existing medical coverage now and start your new life on the right foot.

Will You Be Less Active?

For those of you contemplating a move to a work-from-home business, this is a good possibility. Thanks to advances in technology, thousands of people have been given the opportunity either to telecommute for their current employers or to launch their own home-based business. While working from home has many advantages, it's important to consider the potential pitfalls as well. Lack of exercise and a loss of social interaction are two factors that could eventually lead to not just weight gain, but depression. Make sure to keep the blues at bay by engaging in regular exercise, preferably through a class. Classes keep you on a regular schedule and provide some measure of accountability. If your only goal is to go to the gym and work out today, you're less likely to follow through than if you know your presence will be missed by others in the class.

If the thought of exercise classes doesn't excite you, there are other options such as joining a hiking club, walking group, bird-watching club, contra dancing class, etc. The idea is to get you away from your computer, get your blood pumping (even just a little), and connect with other people.

The Importance of a Clean Bill of Health

In Chapter 4, we looked at the importance of a strong financial foundation; without this, everything else will suffer, including your physical and emotional well-being. Some of you might argue that instead, it's good health that is the cornerstone of a well-balanced life. This is certainly true, because even if you have everything else going for you, it doesn't mean a thing if your health fails. Still, in today's world of rising health costs, finances retain the top slot because of the tremendous financial burden unexpected illness or injury can add to your budget, even with a good health plan. Anyone who has had any kind of surgery understands that the 20 percent most health insurances don't cover can add up to an exorbitant amount.

Your body is like a machine: it requires regular diagnostics and maintenance in order to avoid costly repairs later on. Do what you can to keep it in great working condition for as long as possible. The best approach is to have any necessary screening done now: mammograms, colonoscopies, a good general checkup. It's better to detect and start treating any issues now than in the middle of launching your new career.

The truth is, all three of the aspects we've looked at so far can be enough to derail not just your career change, but your life. Physical Health, Emotional Well-Being, and Financial Soundness are like the three legs of a tripod. Take the time now to ensure each is well balanced.

Health Insurance Options

Access to health care tends to become a hot topic during the election cycle but always seems to get lost in the shuffle afterward. Nevertheless, perhaps one day soon some type of universal coverage will be available. Until then, most people branching out into their own business have to face very high rates for private insurance plans, as well as exclusions or denials stemming from pre-existing conditions.

That said, there are several things you can do to keep your costs lower. First, as stated throughout this chapter, try to get in good shape. Healthy people are cheaper to insure. This goes for smoking, too. If you smoke, now is the time to quit (before the stresses of running your own business further contribute to your habit). Second, you may consider applying for health coverage through a group or organization. The National Association of the Self-Employed offers group plans, as do Realtors' organizations, writer's groups, etc. It will be pointed out many times in this book that as you're investigating your career, it's a great idea to find your industry's related association and to extract as many benefits as possible from membership. This also applies to health care coverage. Finally, if group coverage is not an option, be sure you shop around for the best possible plan, and find the right balance between the size of the monthly payment and overall deductible.

Do You Need a Makeover?

Unless you're embarking on a career change that involves working exclusively from home with internet-only clients, now may be the perfect time to take a good hard look at your physical appearance. Whether you're a younger worker who could use a style upgrade or an older worker needing to convey vitality and energy, don't underestimate the effect your appearance will have on your future success.

Actually, Looks Do Matter

This is especially true for those of you applying for jobs in your new career (as opposed to working for yourself). However, looking your best is also a good idea for those of you starting up your own businesses: If you are lucky enough to land that first client meeting, your looks should inspire confidence.

Blondes may not really have more fun, but studies prove that attractive people are generally favored more by others, even in the job market. This is due to the "halo effect," when people assume that if someone is attractive, then they have other good qualities as well (such as higher intelligence and trustworthiness). Conversely, unattractive people are often associated with negative characteristics.

Regardless of your age, you should ensure that your professional image is one that inspires confidence. You won't need ten new designer suits; just make sure that the clothes you do own are clean and fit you well. You might consider having some of your existing clothes tailored; even inexpensive suits look great when they have been fitted to your body.

The younger you are, the higher the chance that you need to carefully consider the impact of current fads on your personal style. If your new career involves the music, art, or entertainment industries, then face piercings, multicolored hair, or the Goth look are probably fine. But if you're pursuing a more traditional career, you should adopt a more traditional look. Having a personal sense of style and individual flair is fine; just don't take it too far.

Fighting Ageism

Ageism is also an unpleasant reality faced by older workers, with the most common perception being that older workers may not have the energy for the job. A survey by AARP revealed that two-thirds of Boomers believe age discrimination is a factor in the workplace, despite laws prohibiting such behavior. Recent studies even suggest that Boomers are discriminating against other Boomers when it comes to hiring! In fact, it's not out of the question for older workers to hear, "Do you think you have the energy for this job?"

While it's certainly not necessary to dye your hair or get plastic surgery, it is important to have a look—and more importantly, an attitude—that conveys energy, motion, and the ability to keep up with the times.

One way to do this is to make sure that your physical appearance doesn't instantly dismiss you as a dinosaur. Do you still have 80's "wings?" Does your wardrobe scream 70's disco? While it's true that some styles seem to come back over and over again, they don't work as well when the clothes are obviously from that era. The key then is not to look *younger*, but to look *ageless*. As much as possible, you want to take age out of the equation. Clean, classic looks have always worked best during job interviews, and still do.

Finally, be sure you're not practicing age discrimination yourself (toward a younger potential boss or client). A smug attitude doesn't look good on anybody.

Now, let's examine the concepts we've looked at in this chapter to see if right now, you feel a career change is truly "worth it" to you. You may find it helpful to write down your thoughts in a notebook or to discuss these issues with your friends or family. As you answer each question, try to think of specific instances to support your opinion.

Checklist | Is It Worth It?

How many of these statements do you agree with?

○ I understand that it may take a considerable amount of physical and emotional energy to see my career change through.

○ I'm willing to invest the time and energy to get into better shape now to avoid crashing and burning later.

○ I have investigated the health insurance options that will be available to me.

○ I understand that as a younger worker, projecting an image of reliability and confidence is more important than looking "hip" or following the latest fad.

○ I understand that as an older worker, I may face discrimination based on my, age, weight, and overall appearance, even though there are laws to prevent these behaviors.

○ I have investigated the health insurance options that will be available to me.

○ I am willing to update not only my technical skills, but also my look and my attitude in order to be perceived in the best possible light by new employers or clients.

If there are any statements you don't agree with, now is the time to carefully analyze the reasons why and determine how much of a roadblock this item represents in your overall plan.

SUMMARY YOU ARE PHYSICALLY PREPARED TO MAKE A CHANGE BECAUSE:

- You understand physical fitness is key to maintaining a high energy level, which is necessary for most career changes.

- You're not going to wait for the New Year to make important resolutions, but rather view your career change as the chance for a whole new you! Goodbye unhealthy habits, hello health and happiness.

- Taking advantage of the benefits you have today can save you from higher medical expenses later and prevent your new career from being derailed by unexpected illness or injury.

- If the possibility exists that you may be less active during your new career (i.e., operating a home-based business), you are prepared to carve out the time for regular exercise and social interaction, preferably by joining a club or class to increase the likelihood you'll follow through.

- Physical Health, Emotional Well-Being, and Financial Soundness are like the three legs of a tripod, and you're prepared to take the time now to ensure each is well balanced.

- Career changes may involve the added burden of discrimination based on your weight, age, or overall appearance, despite the letter of the law. You are prepared to face these issues head on and are confident that your skills and winning, energetic attitude will win over new potential employers and clients.

CHAPTER 6

Preparing Your Family

If you're like most people, embarking on a career change won't just mean changing your own life, but like a pebble in a pond it will cause a ripple effect touching all those who love you. It's important that your family understands what your goals are, why you want to make a change, and what benefits the entire family can expect from this change. The negative impact on your family should also be discussed in advance and will vary depending on how drastic a change you'll be making, if additional schooling is required, and if you'll be spending a considerable amount of time away from home.

How Will Your New Career Affect Your Loved Ones?

Chances are good that if you're considering a change to doing what you love full-time, your family is on board with the idea. If they're not, they may just need time. "If you're doing what makes you fulfilled and happy, people will adjust," says personal coach (and successful career-changer) Sunny Schlenger.

While it should be relatively easy to sell your family on the positives of switching careers to do what you love, there are certain negative factors that you need to be sure to address up front:

- Will your family experience a significant loss of income from the transition? If so, are they comfortable cutting back on luxury items in exchange for a happier you?
- Will your income go from a regular paycheck to a more uncertain schedule (i.e., commission-based or seasonal work only)? If so, can your family handle the uncertainty?
- Will pursuing your career at this time place an additional burden on your partner? How long is your mate willing to make this sacrifice for you? If you're thinking two years and your partner is thinking three to six months, you need to bring these diverging beliefs in line with reality.
- Will you be less available to extended family, and if so, is your immediate family willing to be a buffer for you? Your partner may be 100 percent on board, but may end up being placed in a position of having to defend your absences at social gatherings or family functions (especially in the short-run).

Going Back to School

One of the biggest obstacles on the path to a successful career change is the effect of your short-term sacrifices on your family. As we discussed in Chapter 5, career changes involve a tremendous amount of energy, both physical and emotional. This is because unless you are suddenly downsized

—which is an increasingly likely possibility these days—you'll need to balance your current job and obligations with all of the activities required to embark on your new career.

If going back to school or obtaining additional training is part of your plan, it's critical that you and your mate take the time to shore up your relationship. Going back to school can negatively impact your relationship, not uncommonly resulting in divorce.

When you think about what is involved in going back to school, you have to factor in several potentially hazardous conditions:

- Long hours away from your mate (or alternatively, spent in front of the computer if you're taking online courses)
- The added financial burden involved (textbooks alone can be a tremendous expense, at over $100 per book on average)
- The feeling of increased social standing, which can be a problem if you will be attaining a higher educational level than your partner
- The threat of infidelity as a result of bonding with classmates while your mate seems less and less relevant

The existence of these potential hazards will not automatically doom your relationship. However, you do need to be aware of these potential pitfalls and take steps now to ensure you won't fall into the quicksand of divorce as a by-product of bettering yourself. Let's look at each of the above factors in detail.

Understand the Time Commitment

Unfortunately, there's usually no getting around the long hours involved in going back to school, whether you are physically commuting to a classroom or taking online classes. In fact, online classes at accredited universities are often more rigorous than on-campus classes, and frequently involve requirements to log in at least three to five days per week.

Also keep in mind that the average college level class requires that you spend two homework hours per one hour of class. A three-credit class translates to six hours of homework and study time each week, in addition to time spent in the classroom.

In addition, adults attending brick-and-mortar classrooms often end up taking evening classes, which can result in schedule that conflicts with your partner's. This could impact your ability to have dinner together, how household chores are handled, your sleep schedules, and both couple and personal (i.e., alone) time.

That said, it's important for you and your mate to make the most of the time you do have together. However small a chunk of uninterrupted time you can carve out with your mate, honor it. Don't let anything take precedence. Even if you can only fit in one hour a week, make that hour as special and as sacred as possible.

Maintain a Team Spirit

It's crucial to keep your mate involved in your progress through clear and inclusive communication. Try to adopt a "we" and not a "me" attitude. As you finish each course, engage in activities/celebrations that make it clear that each course you successfully navigate brings you both closer to reaching the ultimate goal of a better life—for both of you. (See Chapter 7 for the importance of a visible milestone chart.)

It's also important to ensure that your communications with your spouse don't begin to take on a preachy tone. "Well, if you'd taken economics, you'd know that . . ." It's not uncommon for partners of adults going back to school to feel some degree of insecurity when their mate pursues higher education. Those with partners studying at technical or career colleges aren't as prone to this tendency as are those whose partners are attaining advanced degrees.

Another way to foster a spirit of unity is to occasionally engage in learning activities together. Perhaps your mate can attend a lecture at your school, or you can both take a noncredit course together. Even something completely unrelated to academia, such as ballroom dancing, can be a way to unwind, spend quality time with your mate, and cement your bond by learning something new together. Learning can actually be a heady experience—and you don't want to only experience that feeling when you're apart from your mate.

Don't Misplace Your Enthusiasm

Finally, be prudent about the relationships you form with your study partners and classmates. It's not uncommon for those attending college or specialized training to fall into the trap of identifying more with their classmates than with their partner at home. It goes without saying that these types of connections can be damaging to your primary relationship, whether or not physical infidelity occurs. That is why the steps we've outlined so far are vital; they will greatly diminish the likelihood of this happening.

In addition, it's important that you and your partner take the time to clearly outline your respective expectations right at the beginning. "I expect to not have the additional burden of housework while I go to school," or "I expect to have dinner together once a week," etc. Be sure these expectations include some "date time" designed to allow you to reconnect as two interesting adults rather than merely as members of the same household. Both of these steps will prevent you from falling into the quagmire of misplaced loyalties.

Lifestyle Changes:
Dealing with Shifting Realities

In addition to the possibility of having to deal with additional schooling or training, virtually all career shifts will involve some type of altered landscape for your family unit. It's easy for individuals switching careers to focus on the benefits of these changes, not realizing that what to them is a benefit may be (at least initially) daunting to their mates and family. There are several scenarios where this is true. Let's start with the most benign.

Your Gain, Their Loss

So you're tired of the long commute and having to wear a tie, but you enjoy your profession. One day you have the idea of operating a home-based business: still doing what you love, but doing it from the comfort of home. Your perception: no more commutes! No more traffic! You can work in sweatpants and take a mid-afternoon nap if the urge strikes you. Best of all, you can sneak out for the occasional round of golf/fishing trip/daytime hike whenever you want to, not just on weekends. Now let's look at this same situation from your spouse's perception: Twice the amount of housework, more grocery shopping (to keep healthy lunch options in the house), loss of alone time since you're always around. The loss of her craft room/junk room to your new office. Having to be quiet while you're on the phone with a client, or worse, suddenly having to take on clerical duties for you (answering the phone, taking messages, etc.). And did we mention loss of alone time (hint, hint)? You should be getting the picture by now. Be sure you've laid out a plan to deal with these types of issues *before* you hang up your shingle!

Schedule Conflicts

Another scenario involves those jobs with irregular schedules: medicine, law enforcement, military careers, social work, etc. Can your family truly adapt to a job that may be immensely fulfilling for you, but may involve sleeping during daytime hours and working at night? Will they understand when you miss important family functions, or have to cut back on entertaining and getting together with friends? It's never too early to start discussing these issues with those who matter most to you.

Dealing with Worry

Alternatively, is your family prepared to deal with the element of danger in some of those careers? You may have always wanted to enter active law enforcement, but your spouse is stressed to the point of illness at the thought of your being harmed. In situations like this, you may have to do some brainstorming on how to have a career in law enforcement that isn't directly in the line of fire. Alternatively, meeting with those already in the field—and their spouses—might serve to allay some of these fears, or at the very least better educate you both; some of your partner's fears may end up being overblown.

Moving Away

If your job involves relocating, you need to ensure that your family is open to the idea of moving. If you have kids, are they still in school? Are they at an age (the last year or two of high school) where moving now would pull the rug out from under them? If you have elderly parents or family members with special needs, will your new town offer the appropriate facilities and services for them? You should open the dialog as early in the process as possible to see if and how your family unit can cope with the change.

Loss of Status

Finally, if your career change involves a downshift to a less stressful but less glamorous job (say from international banker to kindergarten teacher), can your mate and family adapt to the downgrading of your social status? Truly? While few would admit it openly, many spouses derive their own sense of value and social standing from their mate's profession, which can leave an unhappy but "successful" person trapped in an unwanted career for years. If this is the case, you may wish to consider counseling, or urge your spouse to explore pursuing his own dreams to achieve fulfillment.

The Role of Your Support Network

We talked about the importance of your personal support network in Chapter 3, but here we're addressing the support you need on behalf of your mate and your relationship. As previously noted, your mate might be asked to shoulder significant burdens as you pave the way for your new career. These include increased reliance on your mate's income, the division of household chores, and your partner's role as a buffer to external demands on your time.

In addition to regularly expressing your appreciation to your mate for these sacrifices, you should also find ways to lessen her load. This is where your extended family and friends can lend their support.

Create a Chore Co-op

To cut down on expenses and time spent on household chores, enroll one or more other families in a weekly cooking co-op. This works best with three or more families, but can also work with just two. Participants simply make extra-large batches of one meal per week, sharing it with the other members of the group. That way, at least one day per week, you and your spouse won't have to worry about meal preparation. (Note: When the spouse whose time is derailed by preparations for a career change is the one who normally cooks in the family, it's important to take a proactive approach to your family's eating habits. Don't fall into the trap of expecting too much from the other partner, or of eating expensive or unhealthy takeout all the time.)

If you have younger children, ask a friend or family member to babysit or take them out occasionally, and return the favor at a later date. Other ideas include combining errands; whenever possible, don't duplicate efforts. As with meal preparation, you can find ways to combine grocery shopping, dry-cleaning runs, etc.

For a Few Extra Dollars

If you don't have family or close friends with whom you can swap these duties, consider investing in services such as grocery delivery, dry cleaners that pick up and drop off your order, etc. The larger the town you live in, the lower the cost of these services. You can also look into personal chef services. These can be surprisingly affordable and you can either use the services of a neighborhood company or an internet-based one. These companies deliver "home-cooked" meals that are ready for your freezer or oven and cost roughly $10 per serving. Most major grocery stores also offer this service, at even more reasonable prices. Finally, some personal chefs will come to your home and prepare a week's worth of food based on your family's specifications and nutritional needs.

Little touches like this go a long way toward easing the burden your career change may be placing on your mate and will help maintain goodwill throughout the (sometimes lengthy) transition period when you are likely to be overburdened yourself.

The Ripple Effect

If you have children or elderly parents (or both) it's important that these members of your family also understand your goal—not just what you are doing, but why. If you are a Baby Boomer, you know full well the pressures of "the Sandwich Generation." You might already be in the position of caring for both children and elderly parents. While your children have a greater chance of adapting and fending for themselves to some degree, you may need to ensure that your parents will not be negatively impacted by your decision. If you've been the primary caregiver, perhaps it's time to shift some of these responsibilities to another sibling, at least temporarily. If that's not possible, look into the possibility of adult day care services (either in-home or on-site).

While each family situation is unique, it's universally true that your family will find it easier to support you if you approach your career change as a team effort.

Now, let's examine the concepts we've looked at in this chapter to see if right now, you feel a career change is truly "worth it" to you. You may find it helpful to write down your thoughts in a notebook or to discuss these issues with your friends or family. As you answer each question, try to think of specific instances to support your opinion.

Checklist | Is It Worth It?

How many of these statements do you agree with?

○ I understand my career change may place short-term burdens on both my spouse and family.

○ I'm willing to find creative ways to mitigate these burdens in order to put my relationships—not my new career—first.

○ I am aware that extended family and friends may be less understanding than my mate about my short-term sacrifices.

○ I am willing to take the time to sit down with those in my family circle to discuss expectations and ways we can provide each other mutual support during the transition.

○ I understand that successful career transitions don't happen in a vacuum, and that I should adopt a "we" not "me" attitude.

○ I can accept that what may be a "benefit" for me may have an opposing effect on my mate. I'm willing to weigh the issues from both points of view.

○ My family and I have discussed the impact of loss of income or status associated with my new career and still feel it's worth moving forward.

If there are any statements you don't agree with, now is the time to carefully analyze the reasons why and determine how much of a roadblock this item represents in your overall plan.

SUMMARY YOUR FAMILY IS PREPARED FOR YOUR CAREER CHANGE BECAUSE:

- They are willing to make temporary (or sometimes even permanent) changes in their lifestyles in order for you to do what you love.
- They understand that, many times, short-term sacrifices are necessary for long-term gain.
- Both sides are willing to adjust their expectations of each other.
- You are all willing to find creative ways to manage responsibilities and to be together.
- If your mate is going to have to shoulder additional responsibility, you will make use of personal or professional networks to minimize his burdens.
- You are ready to be protective of your relationship and family unit as you move forward.

PART TWO

Taking the Plunge

Congratulations! If you've made it this far, you have obviously decided that you're ready—emotionally, physically, and financially—to embark on your Journey to Success. You've passed the "Reality Checks" and are prepared to lay the foundation, brick by brick, of your path to the future.

Part 2, "Taking the Plunge," will provide you with the framework to craft a customized plan: one that will serve you not just for switching careers, but for the rest of your life. As you work through the information in each of these chapters, it's a great idea to keep a journal or notebook nearby to write down your ideas. By the end of Part 2, you'll have the outline of a fully realizable plan, ready to go!

CHAPTER 7

Create a Written Plan

As Henry David Thoreau stated, "If one advances confidently in the direction of his dreams, and endeavors to live the life which he has imagined, he will meet with a success unimagined in common hours."

To march confidently in the direction of your dreams, you'll need but one tool: a written plan or "roadmap." Having a written plan with measurable milestones is perhaps the most important piece of advice in this book. Certainly, it is the difference between a pipe dream and a success story!

Why a Written Plan Is Important

For the last ten years, Claire has had a dream: She wants to open her own organic body care shop. "The idea came to me in a dream one night, and I woke up feeling really excited." For the past twenty years, Claire has worked as a hairstylist and masseuse, and her hands and body are now suffering the consequences of prolonged repetitive motion. Opening her body care shop would fulfill her desire to remain in the healing arts, engage her creative juices, and allow her the freedom to work for herself as opposed to working long hours on her feet for someone else.

However, Claire does not have a written plan. She knows what she'd like to do and even what she'd name her business, but the rest are all "fuzzy details." Unfortunately, this has prevented Claire from making any progress whatsoever toward her goal. Each time she suffers a personal setback or unexpected financial expense, she finds herself backpedaling further and further away from her goal. Since initially declaring her goal, she has taken on part-time jobs at retail stores, invested in land, worked as a security guard, and driven a school bus. She is no closer to opening her shop today than she was ten years ago, and at fifty, is not getting any younger. Unless she creates and writes down a specific plan, Claire's body care shop is likely to remain a pipe dream.

Fear of Failure

Most people tend to be like Claire. They have a dream of a better life, but they have no real grasp of how to achieve it. Though they claim to desire change in their lives, they also fear it. Fear of change falls into one of two categories: fear of failure and fear of success. Following one's dream often involves a great deal of personal sacrifice. Frequently, we must give up many of the things that are familiar to us, with only the hope of gaining something better.

Think of your life as a house. You know there is more to life than the room you are currently in, a place where you can experience passion, joy, and fulfillment. Your current room is comfortable, but if you stay there, you will spend your entire life wondering "What's on the other side of that door?" Or worse, "I know a better life awaits outside that door." So what's the problem? You walk to the door, open it, and find a darkened hallway. You know for a fact that there are other doors just a few feet away; you can even see their outlines. What frightens you is the darkened hallway itself. "What obstacles are out there that I can't see?" Suddenly, you decide that you prefer the familiarity of the old room, even though you're not really happy there. The pattern repeats itself, and this room is where you will spend your entire life, too fearful to venture out. This scenario epitomizes fear of failure.

A written, executable plan, on the other hand, is like a flashlight. While there will always be some degree of uncertainty in life, you will be able to see the steps directly in front of you, making it far easier to step right up to—and fling open—the door to your new life.

Fear of Success

The other fear people have is actually achieving their goal, or fear of success. "Why would anyone fear success?" you might wonder. There are several reasons. According to Paulo Coelho, world-renowned author of *The Alchemist*, the primary reason is guilt. "We look around at all those who have not achieved what they want and feel that we do not deserve success either." According to Coelho, this is the most dangerous of all obstacles, because it carries with it a "saintly aura."

Another reason people fear achieving their goals is that they are afraid the reality will not match the dream. Using the metaphor of the house, they are afraid once they cross that darkened hallway and open the door to their new life, they may not like it. And it may be impossible to turn back.

That is why, in addition to tangible milestones, a good written plan will also provide for the elimination of uncertainty, as well as a good exit strategy if the dream doesn't match expectations.

Teresa's *Story*

Formerly a stay-at-home mom, Teresa wanted to become a teacher. Not just any teacher, but a teacher for the Department of Defense schools abroad. This would allow her and her family to travel the world, as well as build her own substantial career to fall back on in case her husband couldn't sustain his role as primary breadwinner. Her husband, Frank, worked in a volatile industry, subject to mergers, acquisitions, and downsizing. In addition, he worked in a high-pressure sales environment, which they did not see as a sustainable career in terms of either health or peace of mind.

The first thing Teresa did was research the requirements for teaching at DoD schools and then find out what made for a competitive advantage. Since she already had a degree in mass communications, she started taking online classes for her master's in education. While she was taking online classes, she also researched the certifications that were the most commonly sought for overseas schools.

At the conclusion of her master's program, she already knew that the next step was to attain individual certifications, and she was also familiar with which states would be the easiest to work with. By the time she actually applied for a teaching position overseas, she had crafted herself into the ideal candidate.

Today, the family is enjoying their first overseas assignment in Turkey, and the kids are getting an education enriched by travel and experiencing new cultures. Frank still works for his company, but should anything change, Teresa has finally established her own credentials for a bright and successful future, wherever the family moves next. Meanwhile, they are living their dream overseas. ●

You too can be more like Teresa than Claire. Just follow the steps in this chapter and you'll be well on your way!

Creating Tangible Milestones

For your goal to one day materialize, you need to first solidify it by putting it in writing. But simply writing down a generic goal is not enough. There are actually four steps to creating an effective written plan.

Clearly State Your Destination

The first step is to succinctly state your goal: "In three years, I would like to own and operate my own pastry shop." Attaching a date is crucial, whether it is one, three, five, or ten years from now.

Assemble the Stepping Stones

The next step is to write down everything you can think of that will be required of you to achieve that goal (i.e., go to culinary school, obtain food and liquor licenses, find a location, etc.). You don't have to worry about listing things in order. For now this is just a brainstorming session. It could actually take several days until you feel your list is fully fleshed out. (Incidentally, this is one area where obtaining the input of others already in the profession will be invaluable. More on this later.)

Lay Out Your Path

The third step is to organize these pieces into chronological order and attach reasonable due dates by each one. Keep in mind that these dates may change as you begin to research your objectives. Don't be discouraged if something takes a bit longer than you originally anticipated. It's also important to constantly update your plan with the correct dates and timelines. The more realistic your plan is, the likelier it is you'll stick to it. Conversely, the more loosely you regard the dates, the less importance you'll attach to achieving those milestones.

Also keep in mind that as you go through this process, it's likely you'll uncover a multitude of mini-milestones that comprise the bigger ones. For example, "Get a culinary degree" is comprised of: "Find a suitable school," "Research tuition," "Investigate grants and scholarships," "Enroll," and "Attend classes." Each of the twenty-four required classes is also a mini-milestone. Be sure you keep your roadmap in sight, and find a way to reward yourself each time you complete a milestone, big or small.

Characteristics of Successful Plans

Successful plans have three characteristics: They complement your thinking and learning style, they are easy to use, and they can be expanded or modified as needed.

It's Right for You

The format of your written plan depends largely on your own preferences and comfort level. Some people are number-oriented; others are concept-driven. Dianne loves working in Excel when it comes to organizing any kind of list. It's how she organizes bills, keeps track of her debt, plans for travel, manages groceries, and almost anything else you can think of. (On the other hand, spreadsheets are anathema to her musician husband.)

Some people, like Mark, prefer flow charts. Mark invested in a large flipchart and stand, which he keeps on display in his home office. His goal is at the top of the chart, which leads to major milestones, which lead to minor milestones. As he completes each minor milestone, he puts a line through it, leaving a visible list of tasks both accomplished and pending.

Anna, who is an artist, developed a colorful Candyland®-type path that depicts her goal at the end of a pathway comprised of little blocks. As she completes each step toward her goal, she puts a colored dot on the appropriate square, thus visually closing the gap between her current status and her dream.

It's Easy to Use

Regardless of the method you choose, be sure it is a) visible and b) easy to update. You could develop the best dream realization software program on Earth, but if you don't view it daily or even weekly, you've just wasted a lot of time. A good way to get around this is to have a detailed plan and a milestone chart. For example, your detailed plan could be in Excel, while your milestones pop up in Outlook when they are due. Alternatively, you could have a fully detailed flowchart on a stand, but mark important completion dates on a desk calendar.

Find a system you are comfortable with, and be faithful to it. Most experts, including Stephen Covey, author of *The 7 Habits of Highly Effective People*, agree that it takes just twenty-one days for a behavior to become a habit. If you can train yourself to view and update your written plan every day for this amount of time, it will become ingrained (and therefore very effective at keeping you on track to your final goal).

It's Comprehensive

Finally, you need to be sure that your original brainstorming session and milestone chart don't just list new tasks, but include the removal of obstacles on the path to success. Examples might be paying down credit card debt and refinancing your mortgage in order to afford these additional responsibilities. Another example might be weight loss or improving your current sleep or exercise habits in order to have more energy for the tasks at hand.

Researching Requirements

As you begin to research the milestones leading to your goal, you are sure to discover multiple requirements that you hadn't previously known existed, let alone considered during your brainstorming session. This is why your plan needs to be easy to update.

Make Use of the Internet

In this day and age, most people are familiar with the basic online search engines, such as Google and Wikipedia. While these sites certainly contain valuable information, you'll be better served by using them to locate expert resources within your field. For example, while you could certainly Google "How to open a pastry shop," you'd be better off searching for "bakers + association" to find the American Bakers Association and then visiting their website. A word about Wikipedia: while this site is certainly extremely informative and contains a lot of information, keep in mind that not all of the articles on this site have been verified. However, most Wikipedia entries do contain links to expert sources for most subject matters.

Local Laws and Resources

Also keep in mind that depending on your chosen career path, requirements are likely to vary by state (and sometimes city or county). In fact, very few career paths have identical requirements across state borders! Therefore it goes without saying that if you're currently living in Maine but are considering a move to Tennessee, be sure you research the right state's requirements.

Hitting the Books

You may also consider a trip to your local library. Gone are the days of the stern librarian rifling through the card catalog. Today's library staff are experienced online researchers, and within minutes are likely to find a wealth of directly relevant information. This could potentially save you hours of sorting through hundreds of irrelevant results. Best of all, much of this information is free!

Also worth considering are books in the *Everything* (*www.everything .com*) series, which cover a wide range of topics—from opening a B&B to starting a dog grooming business and beyond.

As we'll see in the next section, one of the best ways to engage in research is through direct networking.

Making the Right Connections

Almost anything you do in life, for business or pleasure, is easier when you have an experienced guide leading the way. For this reason, one of the very first tasks on your list should be to locate people currently living out some version of your dream career. There are multiple ways to do this.

Social Networking Sites

Once again, the Internet is an excellent source. Social networking sites, such as LinkedIn and Facebook, are great for making initial introductions. Other sites, such as Meetup, are focused more on getting offline and meeting in groups. Groups exist for almost every idea you can think of, from working-mom support groups to amateur photography critique sessions. If the particular group you're looking for doesn't exist, you can also start your own group.

Your Current Circle

Second, don't hesitate to use your existing network to find new friends or mentors. For example, if you're interested in setting up your own photography studio, but don't personally know any professional photographers, send an e-mail to your existing friends and family asking them for their contacts. More times than not, you'll receive some useful contacts in this fashion, which might be more comfortable for you than using online social networking programs.

Speak Your Dream into Existence!

Another good habit to get into is to announce your goal to everyone you meet (unless, of course, they are connected to your current job). This should be easy since most conversations among strangers start out with some form of a "What do you do?" exchange. Simply get into the habit of modifying your response to include your future aspiration. Instead of saying, "I'm an engineer," try, "I'm currently an engineer, but I'm in the process of transitioning to a new career in public politics because I'm concerned about my town's water supply." You might be surprised at some of the interesting (and useful) conversations this technique will spark.

Join the Pros

As the time draws nearer to realizing your goal, join a professional networking group for your career, even if it's just at an associate membership level. These groups will not only save you the time and trouble of learning the basics on your own, but they may also provide you with possible job opportunities or potential client pools.

The Importance of a "Trial Run"

Somewhere in your written plan, you need to factor in a "trial run," whereby you can test the waters of your new career without fully committing. It's important that this aspect of the plan take place early on, before you've invested a significant amount of time, money, or resources toward your goal. This step is so important that an entire chapter has been devoted to exploring it (Chapter 8: "Stick Your Big Toe In: The Trial Run"). Depending on the outcome of your trial run, you will then either be motivated to modify your dream, drop it altogether in favor of another idea, or move full steam ahead. The trial run is what will ensure that the light at the end of the tunnel isn't an oncoming train.

SUMMARY CREATING A WRITTEN PLAN FOR YOUR NEW CAREER IS VITAL BECAUSE:

- A written plan is what distinguishes a pipe dream from future success.
- Accomplishing minor milestones will keep you motivated and on track.
- A written plan can help eliminate fear of failure.
- Dedicating the time, thought, and effort to craft a written plan will bring to light challenges that might otherwise be revealed too late.
- Roadmaps provide a visual reminder of your progress, which can keep you motivated when times are tough.
- Brainstorming sessions will not only identify future tasks, but current obstacles that may be weighing you down.
- A solid roadmap will also include important connections to your future colleagues and clients.
- A well-crafted plan will incorporate a trial run, as well as a viable exit strategy. The earlier in the plan the trial run, the cleaner the exit.

CHAPTER 8

Stick Your Big Toe In: The Trial Run

As we've briefly touched on before, embarking on a new career path can involve multiple other changes: in your location, in the people you deal with on a daily basis, in your daily duties and responsibilities, in how both you (and others) perceive yourself, and in the lives of those you love. This chapter will show you how to realistically evaluate the impact of these changes, before your dream turns into a nightmare.

Dream or Nightmare? One Possible Scenario

To fully appreciate the importance of a trial run, take a moment to imagine the following scenario. Fast-forward your life to approximately one year (or more) into the future. You've successfully followed all of the steps in this book: You've prepared yourself physically, emotionally, mentally, and financially. Perhaps you've even gone back to school for a certification, license, or new degree. Your spouse or significant other is on board. You've spent a considerable amount of time networking for your new career. Most likely, you've even successfully downsized your household or transferred locations altogether.

Then the big day arrives: your first day on the job. Strangely, there are no heralding trumpets, no ticker-tape parade. You're nervous and excited, but you plunge forth. A day passes, then a week. After a month, you find yourself overcome by the discoveries you've made about your new life and career. After two to three months (long enough for the immediate "newness" to wear off), you make the most important discovery of all: you don't like it. How do you go back? At this point, you likely feel as if you can't. You've invested your heart, soul, and savings into this change, and perhaps your partner has as well. For many people, this is the end of the road; their dream has turned into a nightmare, and the road out is blocked by the stumbling blocks of pride, poor planning, or both.

Jumping into a new career is akin to jumping into an unknown river. It may look beautiful and inviting from a distance, but you'll really have no idea of what it will be like until you become immersed in it. Sticking your big toe in—taking a trial run—allows you the opportunity to test the waters first. Sometimes, you may discover immediately that the new environment is not as inviting as it seemed from a distance. Other times, it will be the motivating push you might need to overcome your fear of change and follow through with your plans. There is only one way to know for sure.

Testing the waters for your new life and career could involve several aspects, all of them important. These include, but are not limited to, location, peers, and daily duties.

Location, Location, Location! How to Really Evaluate Your Potential New Home

If your new career will require a change of venue, it's important to spend some time visiting the new location. How the local chamber of commerce or current residents portray the location may not be at all how you perceive it. If it's someplace that you have never lived (or alternatively, have not lived there in a long time), this is especially important. Memories of previous homes, especially if they are childhood or early adult memories, can be deceiving. (Not to mention that with the rapid pace of growth and industrialization, your hometown may have changed beyond recognition.)

Love at Second, and Third, Sight

It's important to schedule multiple visits to the new location. Be sure that these visits are not during the "prime time" for that area, when it will be looking its best. February tends to be a great month for evaluating a potential new residence; most areas are at their worst during this month, with the exception of places like Florida (when it's possibly at its best). It's fairly easy to look up an area's climate information; find the least appealing month and then plan your visit for that time. It's better to discover you can't handle the stresses of hurricane season while you're on a short vacation in Florida than after you've bought a new oceanside property there! Or that the charming town in Maine that you visited in July last year changes character completely in February.

Don't Be a Tourist

During your visit, try to stay in accommodations other than hotels. Short-term house rentals (or even time-shares) work well. Rather than ordering room service and living a vacation lifestyle, you'll be shopping in the local stores, interacting with the local people, and experiencing the traffic patterns. After all, that's what you'd be doing if you actually lived there.

Dig for Inside Information

When scouting out a new location, organizing visits is only one part of testing the waters. Consider subscribing to the local paper (or bookmark it on your computer for daily visits), and do plenty of other research. Before making a move, you should investigate the cost of living (housing and food prices), taxation rates, impact fees, and crime rates. Infrastructure and transportation are also key. Is it easy to get in and out? Will you feel isolated from friends and family? Will it be difficult geographically to establish or access your support network?

You should also determine local licensing requirements for your new career, as well as the number of employment opportunities, size of the client pool, and existing competitors.

It's Who You Know:
Meeting Your Future Peers and Clients

Unless the type of career change you are contemplating involves working in total seclusion (such as an Internet-based endeavor) it will be important to determine your compatibility with your future peers and clients.

If you're working as an accountant today, but believe you'd do well in the hospitality industry, it's important to spend time away from the world of Excel spreadsheets and calculators and experience firsthand what it's like to meet your clients across the width of a counter, when they're tired, hungry, or have other demands. Or maybe you're tired of your career in academia and want a job working in the great outdoors, perhaps at a nursery or landscaping company. Your peers will likely have educational backgrounds, values, or work ethics that differ widely from those of your former colleagues. In fact, you may initially have more in common with the client who comes in to buy plants for his backyard than you do with your new coworkers. Will you feel comfortable bridging that gap? Will you feel comfortable in your new persona?

Not "As Seen on TV": What Your Daily Duties Will Really Be Like

Thanks to bestselling novels and television shows, most of us have a glamorized view of many careers, most notably chefs, doctors, medical examiners, and private investigators. Usually, the reality of these jobs differs significantly from what is portrayed across these media.

Fiction: The chef can be seen artfully stirring a sauce, adding a sprig of herbs, and coming out to accolades from his diners. Fact: Chefs spend an inordinate amount of time on their feet, hovering over steaming-hot pans, after getting up early and going to bed late. Complaints outnumber compliments on most days. Fiction: The medical examiner comes out to examine a body and finds a clue that proves this is another victim of a feared serial killer. Fact: Most medical examiner work is done on people who have died of natural or mundane causes, and most of their time is spent in their offices. Fiction: The private investigator is paid an exorbitant fee to follow a client's paramour, who turns out to be an international jewel thief on the lam from Interpol. Fact: Most private investigation work these days is done via computer. Stakeouts are usually only required when working on cases involving adultery or bogus accident or workmen's compensation claims. Stakeouts are also lengthy, tiresome, and—dare I say it—boring.

The Importance of a Short-Term Immersion

The best way to test the waters in cases like these is to try a short-term immersion. There are many different methods: taking on a part-time job in your chosen industry, applying for an internship or apprenticeship, or going on a "ride-along" with someone currently in the profession you're aspiring to. There are even companies offering short-term immersion working "vacations" where you can test out a new career.

Get a Part-Time Job

Obtaining a part-time job in your chosen career is perhaps the easiest of these options. Regardless of the type of career you're considering, from hospitality to law enforcement to medicine, there are plenty of opportunities to get a firsthand glimpse of what these worlds are really like. Naturally, you may not be able to find a job doing exactly what you'd be doing down the road, but you can at least get to know the types of people you'd be interfacing with in your new career. The beauty of the part-time job approach is that it is the simplest to begin—and end, if you so desire.

The Apprentice

On the other end of the spectrum are internships and apprenticeships, which, depending on your chosen career, may be more appropriate choices. Internships and apprenticeships may be more difficult to obtain, but they are useful in that they provide some level of on-the-job training, and you can begin to get a glimpse of what your dream job's daily duties are really like. Some careers—such as housing appraisers—actually require a significant number of apprenticeship hours as part of your formal application process.

Along for the Ride

Another option is to be a spectator for a day, or a weekend. This is easiest to accomplish when you know someone who is already working in your desired field. Ride-alongs are best known as a technique for authors and journalists desiring a firsthand look at law enforcement, but there's no reason one can't apply the same method to other careers. (Note: This is not the same thing as watching a so-called "reality" show or realistic drama on television. Boring does not sell, so rest assured that even "reality" shows have been pared down and edited to show only the most riveting portions.)

When arranging a ride-along, be sure that your host has cleared it with his superiors. Since this is a benign request—"Joe is contemplating a career change to nursing and wants to see what a day in the life at the hospital is like"—you shouldn't face too many barriers. It's also helpful to arrange more than one ride-along, with a few different hosts. That way, you'll be able to clearly see which aspects of the job are universal and which ones are unique to a particular employer or situation.

Know When to Fold 'Em: Why You Shouldn't Leave Your Current Job — Yet

As should be apparent by now, changing careers can involve a significant amount of cost, especially if further schooling or licensing is required or if a change of location is in order.

So for one thing, embarking on a mini test drive of your new career while still ensconced in your old job will provide you with both a financial cushion and the security of reliable income.

It's also possible that by participating in ride-alongs, taking on a part-time job in a related field, or completing an internship, you may discover that the career of your dreams isn't what you really want. If this happens, you'll have the luxury of re-evaluating your next step from familiar territory. If, on the other hand, you love your new career choice, you've missed out on nothing but unnecessary risk.

Options for an Extended Vacation, Leave of Absence, or Sabbatical

Depending on whether your new career will involve a new location (perhaps even a new country!), extensive schooling, or a significant financial investment, it may be prudent to undertake a more concentrated immersion than discussed above. The bigger the risk you'll be undertaking, the longer and more in-depth your test drive should be.

Working Vacations

As discussed previously, potential new locations should be visited on multiple occasions, preferably in the off-season and during unattractive times. In addition, it is often instructive to visit your new location while involved in the type of work you plan to be doing.

Even if you're not planning on moving, you may wish to conduct your test drive in a different location in order to more fully immerse yourself in your "new life." If you live in a small town or community, this may also be the best way to avoid concern at your office about why you're working as an intern for another company.

Three Choices

Depending on your chosen industry, you can find internships and volunteer opportunities all over the world for two-week stints. Be aware that most volunteer opportunities may also involve a cost to you to cover food, lodging, and training. Some of these volunteer organizations are listed in the online Resource Appendix (go to: *www.unplugyourhead.com/dowhatyoulove* for more info).

Opportunities also exist to negotiate with individual business owners for a test drive. For example, if you're considering a career in hospitality, you might be able to persuade the owner of a B&B to exchange some sweat equity (yours) for a reduced rate and a behind-the-scenes education. Sites such as craigslist are excellent for these types of purposes.

If your time is limited and you lack the courage to propose this type of arrangement to a business owner, consider a matching service. Companies such as VocationVacations (*www.vocationvacations.com*) allow you to test-drive your chosen career for a predetermined period. Keep in mind that these services can be expensive (roughly $1,000 for a two-day immersion and mentoring program, not including most meals or lodging).

Extended Leave or Sabbaticals

If your test drive is short (two days to two weeks) arranging a vacation shouldn't be a problem. However, if your new career will be taking you overseas, you'll realistically need longer than two weeks to fully evaluate both a new career and a new location. In those cases, applying for a leave of absence or a sabbatical would be the recommended approach.

If you're lucky enough to work for a company with an existing sabbatical program, you shouldn't need to detail your exact plans or intentions. If you're going to apply for a leave of absence, you'll need to think very carefully about how to present your request, and if it has the potential to endanger your current position. I discuss this topic at length in *Unplugged: How to Disconnect from the Rat Race, Have an Existential Crisis, and Find Meaning and Fulfillment* (Sentient, 2008).

SUMMARY YOU SHOULD TEST-DRIVE YOUR CAREER BEFORE TAKING THE PLUNGE BECAUSE:

- Your new career could involve significant investments of time, money, and resources. It could also mean downsizing and other sacrifices on the part of your family. It's better to test the waters than to jump into an unknown river.

- Your new career could involve relocation, and it's true that "location is everything." Visit potential new locations during nonprime season for the most realistic evaluation.

- Your new career will mean new colleagues, clients, and bosses. Establishing your compatibility with all three is a vital step on the path to future job satisfaction.

- Life isn't like television. Even "reality" shows contain misinformation, and all are edited to leave out the "boring parts." Be sure you can handle all aspects of your new career: the exciting and the boring.

- Trial runs allow you to keep the security of your current job, which will give you the luxury of re-evaluating your next move if the trial run proves a disaster.

- There are many ways to embark on a trial run: extended vacations, leaves of absence, and sabbaticals. Choose the one that works best for you!

CHAPTER 9

The Water's Fine: Taking the Plunge

If, after your trial run, you decide that you would definitely like to proceed with your career change, there are several things you need to keep in mind, though you may be tempted to give notice immediately and plunge headfirst into your new life.

Before You Dive In

Back to the river analogy: sticking your big toe in is not the same as being fully immersed and wearing waterproof goggles. While you may have an increased level of comfort regarding the new job, throwing caution to the wind and plunging in headfirst may result in hitting a hidden rock. On the other hand, you don't want to spend the rest of your life waiting indecisively on the riverbank. The solution? Don't forget your written plan!

Back to the Plan

Remember, every step of your journey should be clearly outlined in your written plan, as discussed in Chapter 7. The trial run is just one more step along the way, and it by no means should be your last step. Transitioning from one career and lifestyle to another is stressful enough; doing so without a clearly defined strategy may add unbearable stresses to your health and relationships.

Take Stock of Your Life

Once you've made the decision to proceed, you should undertake an immediate assessment of your current situation. Are your finances in order? Is your debt under control? Is there anything at all from your current career that is still outstanding in terms of benefits you'll need to move forward? Be sure that at this point, you've worked through each of the checklists in Chapters 3 through 6 and have addressed each of those concerns. You will not be ready to take the plunge until you've done so.

Spread the Word

As part of your plan, you will have already joined the appropriate networking groups for your chosen career. Now is the time to let it be known that you are ready to take advantage of new opportunities. Put the word out to everyone in your networks (both personal and professional) that you are looking for a job/launching your business/seeking clients, etc.

One mistake people often make at this point is to sound as if they are already successful: "I'm pleased to announce the launch of my new business, XYZ Consulting . . ." followed by what should be advertising copy. Instead, when reaching out to your networks for the first time, don't be afraid to ask for help: "I'm excited to launch my new business and am searching for new clients! Do you know someone who could use the services of a personal chef?" Or, "I just completed my teacher's certification. Do you know of any current openings at your school?" The door to Opportunity is sometimes propped open by a friend. Make sure you don't waste your time knocking on locked doors instead.

A Soft Place to Land

Although finances were discussed at length in Chapter 4, one aspect bears mentioning here. In addition to making sure your finances are generally in order, you should also make sure that you have a suitable buffer (minimum of three months of living expenses) standing by. This is true whether you're hanging up your own shingle or applying for a new job. Even if your plan is to hold onto your current job until you've secured a job with a new employer, it's still wise to have a buffer.

For one thing, having a buffer will go a long way toward calming any feelings of misapprehension and second-guessing that are typical of career-changers in the first few months. A buffer will give you the feeling that a clean exit is still possible, should you so desire. Contrast this with starting your new job knowing that every penny counts. Even if you find yourself enjoying the job, you are still likely to feel somewhat "trapped" by your financial obligations.

Why You Shouldn't Burn Your Bridges

There are two very good reasons why you shouldn't burn your bridges upon leaving your current employer, both of them involving your reputation.

References Matter

If you are launching your own business, finding enough new clients to be able to transition to full-time status should be your first goal. If you're seeking a position with a new employer, priority one should be crafting an attractive resume. In either case, however, you will need solid references. For this reason alone, it's important to stay on good terms with your current employer. If possible, you should leave on good enough terms that obtaining a written recommendation from one or more of your end users won't be a problem.

Just in Case

Another reason you should leave on good terms is in case of the unthinkable—that someday you may need to return to your present occupation. Even if your old job isn't available, your old network could still be a source of potential opportunities. Your former boss and coworkers are more likely to recommend you than if you went out in an ill-thought-out blaze of glory.

Finally, don't forget that it's a small world out there, and even if your new career is going swimmingly, you never know whom your potential clients or new boss might run into at a cocktail party.

Till Death Do You Part: A Plan for Life

From the moment you first laid pen to paper (or fingers to keyboard) and turned your fantasy into a black-and-white plan, you've been laying the groundwork for success, one milestone at a time. Just because you're about to cross the threshold to your dream doesn't mean it's time to leave your roadmap behind.

For many of you, the system you've been using to chart your progress has not only become ingrained, it's something you actually look forward to. As you venture forth into your new career, it's strongly advisable to use the same system that brought you this far to help set new milestones for continuing success. Even dream jobs lose some of their shine eventually, but a good written plan can help keep you motivated and looking forward to the future for years to come. Furthermore, a good plan can be applied to other areas of your life, including your personal and family goals in addition to your career.

Develop a Professional Presence

If you're launching your own business, the first thing you'll need to do is establish a professional presence. We'll look at three components: online, paper, and portfolio.

Your Online Presence

In today's world, no business can do without a website. A word of caution: make sure your website is professional. Even a one-page, sharp-looking site is better than one that looks as if it were assembled by your "cousin's wife's brother-in-law." It's a strange aspect of the modern mindset that we are quick to judge a business by its website, yet no one wants to spend money on his own website. "I know someone who does websites," can be a dangerous thing to hear. Remember: you get what you pay for. (Check the Online Resource Appendix if you're in need of a site.)

Cards, Letterhead, and Logo

The same goes for professional-looking business cards, letterhead, and a logo. Part of your expense in setting up your new business identity should be having a graphic designer create a unique logo for you. Use this on everything, from your website to your letterhead to your business cards. The goal is to create a unified "brand" that communicates professionalism and confidence.

Speaking of cards: spend a few extra dollars and order quality business cards. Long after you've walked away from a meeting, your card remains as the only visible reminder of you and your business. Make sure it's a positive association. Cards created on an inkjet printer just don't have the same impact, no matter how much the technology has improved over the last few years.

Your Portfolio

Finally, here's a tip for adding a feeling of substance and reliability to a new business website. Rather than listing "Clients" (of whom you're likely to have none), create a heading called "Clients/Experience." Here you can list all of your old employers, giving potential clients a feeling of assurance that they're dealing with a professional. Naturally, you don't want to misrepresent yourself to anyone who inquires about exactly what you did for the Widget Factory, but you'd probably be surprised at how few people will ever question your list.

Craft a Suitable Resume

For those seeking employment in a new industry, the same principle applies to your resume: It's the first impression of you potential employers will have.

Functional Resumes

Typical resumes (chronological accounts of your career history) are often not the best suited to career changers. Instead, you may wish to adapt a "functional" format, which showcases your related skills and interests, with a chronological list of positions held at the end. To create this format, lead with a career goal and qualifications summary, and then create functional categories that highlight your related skills and experience. For example, if you're applying for a job as a corporate trainer, you'd want to choose "training experience," "team leadership," and "presentation skills" as your categories. Be sure that your format isn't so difficult to follow that employers lose interest or become suspicious of any gaps.

Pros and Proofreaders

That said, it might not hurt to spend a few extra dollars to have a professional craft a functional or combination functional/chronological resume for you. You can find resume writing experts—as well as see online samples of different styles—on job boards such as Monster.com.

If you choose to write your resume yourself, be sure you have several people read it for clarity and to check for errors. Remember, you won't have a second chance to make a first impression!

SUMMARY NOW IS THE TIME TO TAKE THE PLUNGE BECAUSE:

- You've tested the waters and they are inviting.
- You've established a solid professional network in your chosen career.
- You'll be leaving on good terms with your old employer.
- You have a significant financial "buffer" to reduce stress and unease.
- You've developed a finely honed written plan to launch you into your new career and beyond.
- You've placed a check mark next to every item in Chapters 3 through 6.
- You've reached out to your personal contacts for help.
- You've created professional and quality-looking promotional materials.
- You can't imagine spending another day waiting to make your dream a reality!

PART THREE

Consider the Options

Maybe you've read the first two parts of this book and are ready to embark on a specific career—the one you've been dreaming of for a long time. Or maybe, you're torn between two or more career choices; you just know that what you're doing now isn't what you want to be doing forever. Whichever scenario applies to you, you can benefit from reading about the real-life experiences of others who've made successful career changes.

The Success Stories in the following chapters have been carefully chosen to illustrate not just the benefits of each career type, but the "pitfalls and perils" as well. (Some chapters even have more than one story, to illustrate how different people can go about pursuing the same general goal in a totally different way.) After all, you want to be sure that your potential new career is really right for *you*, while also ensuring that you don't make preventable mistakes. We'll look at fifteen general categories; feel free to read one chapter or all of them! Each one contains valuable insights that just might make a huge difference for you!

CHAPTER 10

More Than a Hobby

For many people, the choice of avenue to pursue for a second career is an easy one: They decide to focus full-time on a beloved hobby. That said, there is a big difference between doing something for love and doing it for money, and the ability to successfully fuse the two can be challenging. It's not uncommon for the stresses of making your hobby profitable to result in a loss of affection for the activity itself. Many things that make great hobbies do not make great second careers. It's important to carefully evaluate your hobby to ensure its sustainability as a career choice.

Photography

Perhaps one of the easiest hobbies to convert to a profession is photography. Many serious amateur photographers have already invested significantly in equipment, or at least enough to get started with their professional careers. There are many potential job opportunities for professional photographers: graphic design shops, the local paper, advertising media such as catalogs and websites, schools, and government agencies. In addition, you can find work as a portrait photographer for a professional studio. There is also a demand for scientific photographers, who take pictures that are used for scientific procedures and medical records. Since industry experience is often required, this makes a great choice for someone with a previous career in medicine or science.

In addition to professional positions such as the above, freelance opportunities abound. You can become a regular contributor to stock agencies, or work as a freelancer for weddings, birthday parties, and special family events.

Professional or Freelance?

Professional positions in photography often require a related degree (photography or journalism), and the job market is very competitive. Freelance photographers don't face such requirements, but they must be sure that they have the financial acumen to run their own business. It's also important for them to have an understanding of intellectual property requirements and copyrights in order to protect their work.

Digital or Print?

The advent of digital photography is also drastically changing the landscape of this career. First, most photography jobs today require some level of comfort and familiarity manipulating digital media. Second, as more and more people gain the skills to work with digital media, demand for professional services—especially for newspapers—is expected to decline.

The Right Fit for You?

Those considering a professional photography career should possess good coordination, eyesight, and creative ability. Additionally, they should have good interpersonal skills, the ability to listen to client needs, and a high level of accuracy. Sometimes, this career also requires carrying heavy equipment through all kinds of terrain and weather.

Turning Pro

If you are interested in moving forward with a professional career in photography, there are three basic factors to consider: your portfolio, your skills, and your network.

Your Portfolio

Your first step should be assembling a portfolio. In today's world, digital portfolios are a necessity. They not only make applying for jobs much easier, but also portray an image of professionalism and a degree of Internet savvy.

Your Skills

Second, you should enroll in photography courses at your local college. While a degree may or may not be necessary for a successful career, having a solid foundation for the basics (lighting, composition, etc.) will. It's also important to take the time to develop a solid foundation for the tools of the trade: not just the digital aspects, but really getting to know the advantages of all of the equipment.

Your Network

Third, you have to put yourself and your work out there. Local camera clubs are great, but so are online forums. Post as much of your work as possible for feedback and critique by other photography enthusiasts. In addition, attend as many social gatherings and mixers as you can for organizations like your local chamber of commerce. In the beginning, you may have to offer to photograph events for free. Do a professional, immaculate job. Make as many contacts as you can. As with every other client-driven business, a successful photography business depends on referrals.

Sports

One of the hardest hobby-to-career conversions, on the other hand, is pursuing a sport. Moving from an amateur golfer to professional status, for example, requires a great deal of funding and financial support. While you are undergoing physical training for your sport, you'll also be busy finding sponsors, which can be a full-time effort in and of itself. There are also very few sports that aren't geared toward those in their more youthful years.

Sport-Related Careers

That said, a career that is an offshoot of the sport you love is often more tenable. Let's explore several possibilities, using golf as an example.

Become an Official

If you love golf, you can get a job with a related organization, such as the USGA. As a rules official, you get to travel to tournaments and have a front-row seat at events throughout the year. The same holds true for other sporting associations, but individual requirements differ. Typically, positions require membership in the governing association, correctable vision, and passing a written test.

Sell It to Others

If you have a prior career in sales, you can also apply for a job as a manufacturer's representative for equipment, which will involve being surrounded by those active in the sport. Careers such as this often provide great perks: seats to major events, discounted products, etc.

Teaching: Become a Pro

If you have the desire to become a golf pro, you'll need to go through the PGA/PGM apprenticeship program. The program is self-paced but requires you to be working full-time in one of the positions designated by the PGA as meeting the "Eligible Employment" requirement. This requirement must be met in order to register for the program. An applicant must have worked a six-month period out of the twelve months prior to application.

The next step is passing the thirty-six-hole Playing Ability Test (PAT). There is a rather complicated formula that determines the exact scores that must be equaled or bettered, but generally, an applicant must play thirty-six holes fifteen strokes over par or better. Finally, after admission into the program, you must work for three years as a PGA apprentice in a position that is sanctioned by the PGA.

Teaching: Own a Franchise

If the road to becoming a PGA professional is too time-consuming or doesn't mesh with your current financial needs, you can become involved in a teaching franchise, such as the one offered by the Professional Golf Teachers Association of America. The group offers a five-day on-site program teaching you to become a golf teacher for driving ranges, corporate events, high schools and universities, and even as a relief teacher for country clubs (although the main pro at country clubs is likely to be PGA certified).

Many of these same concepts can be applied to other sports, such as tennis. The best source for information is the sport's governing association.

Other Tangential Careers

Those who enjoy outdoor sports (fishing, hunting, canoeing, hiking, etc.) can pursue tangential careers in either outdoor recreation or with governmental groups such as the U.S. Forest Service or the Park Service. Private nonprofits such as the Sierra Club and Outward Bound also offer plenty of opportunities for those seeking jobs in the great outdoors. In addition, groups offering wilderness and camping expeditions are growing in popularity as corporate team-building events, spawning their own adventure job sector.

Crafts

A second career pursuing your craft of choice can be a volatile experience. While most crafts make for easy home-based businesses (jewelry-making, scrapbooking, quilts, painting, etc.), the demand for these items is very volatile. In addition to feeling the pinch when the economy suffers, this career choice is also affected by fads: Scrapbooking may be in one year and out the next.

Production Choices

Another factor to consider when choosing a craft-based business is the ability to find a balance between the appropriate quantity and price to justify increased production. If you only make a handful of quilts per year, you'd have to charge a significant amount for each one you produce to justify it as a "career" and not a hobby. However, unless you are exceptionally talented at what you do and well known within your community, people may not be willing to pay the higher price.

Get Your Product Out There

To be successful at your business, it's vital to make use not just of local art bazaars and craft shows, but to get your products carried by places that do not carry a lot of similar items. Back with the quilt example, you can arrange to have them hang in cafés or places like libraries or hospital gift shops with tags that clearly state that the items are for sale. The best thing to do is to form a relationship with a local business that will mount a small display of your items in exchange for a commission.

Other options for promoting your business include offering to teach adult-education classes at community colleges or similar venues. Finally, consider using the Internet to expand your business not just nationally, but globally as well. It could make the difference between earning enough revenue to survive and having to go back to treating your work as a hobby.

Music

A full-time professional career in music is very difficult to attain, at least at the level of a recording or performing artist. While it was never an easy industry to break into in the first place, these days the entire process has become extremely commercialized and opportunities limited by the decreasing number of labels. A full-time venture into a career as a performing or recording artist would require an entire book focused solely on that topic.

Career Options for Music Lovers

That said, for those who love music but do not have aspirations of grandeur, there are plentiful career options. Paid professional positions include: teaching in public and private secondary schools, music director, conductors of church choirs or community music organizations, and post-secondary music educators. Colleges and universities require at least a master's degree in music, although a doctorate is preferred.

Music Therapists

A new and burgeoning career choice is that of music therapist. In this career, you will combine music, teaching, and therapy to help persons with disabilities improve their physical and mental health. Competent therapists possess not just great musical ability, but emotional stability and insight. Jobs for music therapists can be found at hospitals and outpatient clinics, schools, mental health centers, nursing homes, and correctional facilities.

Reviewers and Writers

Additional paid professional careers include music reviewers for newspapers, instrument repair, managers and booking agents, disc jockeys and radio program directors, and music software programmers. There are also decent paying opportunities for those willing to tour with performing groups as instrument tuners and technicians.

Freelancing

Freelance opportunities to work with music are limited only by your imagination. Freelance musicians most commonly work as performing artists for local clubs, cruise ship and resort entertainers, studio musicians, and home-based music instructors for individual clients.

PITFALLS AND PERILS One of the biggest perils you could encounter with a craft-based business is the risk that the IRS will treat it as a hobby. This could mean the loss of the ability to deduct expenses as business expenses. Unlike hobby expenses, business expenses are fully deductible. If the direct costs of doing business exceed your income from the business, you can use the resulting loss to offset other income reported on Form 1040. If the IRS decides that your new career is really a hobby, these expenses will be subject to a 2 percent floor on Form 1040, Schedule A, meaning they can only be deducted to the extent they exceed 2 percent of adjusted gross income. Furthermore, they cannot exceed your income from the hobby. If you consistently lose money from year to year, the IRS will have grounds to consider your work a hobby.

Most hobby-based businesses have another thing in common: They require a significant amount of back-up cash to draw from as you build your business. This is especially true for product-based ventures since it takes time to gain distribution. If at all possible, it's a good idea to start your hobby-based business part-time while still working in your previous career. This way, when the time comes to transition to full-time work, you won't be in an awkward financial position (and prone to getting discouraged).

For any business to succeed, a business plan is essential. Many people converting their hobbies into professions don't seem to realize this important fact, though it's the one critical element for success. Having a love for what you do is not enough; you need to carefully create a plan that encompasses the business—not just the creative—aspects of the job.

Finally, converting a hobby to a profession has another danger: that the stresses of earning a living may diminish the joy the activity originally brought you. Painting for relaxation and pleasure is different from having to churn out dozens of professional portraits. Making a quilt for a grandson is different from mass-producing them for a gallery. Teaching your brother how to improve his swing is different than teaching student after student after student at a driving range. ●

SUCCESS STORY

In 1981, Tom was one of the many thousands of air traffic controllers to be laid off by the Reagan administration after the strike. Initially, he stayed in Minnesota and pursued a secondary career in aviation working for Northwest Airlines.

Tom and Mary had known each other their entire lives, as they were loosely related and often ended up at the same family functions. They became friends after the death of her husband, when he gave her a book of poetry to help her through the grieving process. Using his job at the airlines, he flew back and forth to Wichita to see her, and the friendship blossomed over the next three years.

Although Mary had been the class photographer in high school and college, it wasn't really her love. A talented sculptor, she'd been working for years in that craft. She'd also found a way to integrate sculpture into her work at a healing arts center, where she had been working as a spiritual counselor.

One day, on a fluke, Tom invited her to go with him on a photography trip to Alaska. She called her daughter and asked, "Do you think I'll be able to stand him for three days in a place like Alaska?" With her daughter's encouragement, she embarked on what would become a life-changing journey.

The two soon developed a joint love for photography and found themselves going on photo shoots to Alaska every quarter. One day they both looked at each other and said, "Let's just move there." They loaded up their possessions and headed north. Once they settled in Homer, they bought a house.

Thanks to Tom's career in the airlines, he had a pension to draw from. Mary also had some residual income from her sculpture business, as well as a pension from her first husband's career in the military. Their accumulated savings enabled them to take a big risk and move to the state they had grown to love.

Marketing is the toughest challenge the duo face. "The artistic stuff doesn't really sell," Tom confides. The couple earns most of their income on commercial photography products and small prints for the tourist trade. "People like to be able to buy a good shot of a bear and claim they took it," Tom chuckles.

When it comes to those considering a full-time photography career, Tom offers this advice: "Think about how much money you need to make and what you love to do. Then find a way to earn enough money doing one thing to support the other."

For example, Tom and Mary use the income they earn from the commercial work they do to support the work they really enjoy doing: photography for wildlife refuges. This work is done on a volunteer basis, but the couple gets an immense amount of satisfaction from using their photography skills to aid conservation efforts. "It's important to document what's out there that needs to be saved," Tom says. "Even if someone never makes it to Alaska, they should know what's there."

At age seventy-two and sixty-five respectively, Tom and Mary have faced their share of challenges operating in this beautiful but harsh new environment. "You haven't had fun until you've had to use an outhouse in twenty below, just because you've got to catch the auroras on a clear cold night," says Tom. "Not to mention lugging loads of heavy camera equipment on icy and remote paths."

In addition to the environment, Tom and Mary have had to get used to the high cost of living in Alaska. "Everything is about 25 percent higher in price than in the lower forty-eight due to shipping costs. You really have to think about what you need and how frequently you should order it." There are some offsets, however. "There is no state income tax. In fact, the state paid me $2,100 just to live here, plus another $1,200 to offset the price of fuel. When you have a couple living here, that doubles to over $6,000."

Despite all of the tests and hardships that their new lifestyle presents, the couple doesn't have a single regret. Well, one: "God, we should have done this twenty years ago!" You can see Tom and Mary's work by visiting *www.wildnorthphoto.com.* ●

Now, let's examine the concepts we've looked at in this chapter to see if, right now, you feel converting your hobby into your career is "worth it" to you. You may find it helpful to write down your thoughts in a notebook or to discuss these issues with your friends or family. As you answer each question, try to think of specific instances to support your opinion.

Checklist | Is It Worth It?

How many of these statements do you agree with?

○ I am able to handle the business aspects of my new career, not just the creative side.

○ Sometimes, doing an activity for profit can reduce or eliminate the pleasure experienced from the hobby. I don't believe this will be true for me.

○ I am willing to explore a variety of ways I can be involved in my chosen industry.

○ I understand the financial and tax implications of making the transition from hobby to business.

If there are any statements you don't agree with, now is the time to carefully analyze the reasons why and determine how much of a roadblock this item represents in your overall plan.

SUMMARY CONVERTING MY HOBBY TO A CAREER IS RIGHT FOR ME BECAUSE:

- I have a strong passion that I would love to dedicate myself to full-time.
- I have the skills to run a small business or to apply to a professional setting working for someone else.
- There are multiple jobs available in the industry I love, although they may be indirectly related.

CHAPTER 11

Starting a Nonprofit

If you're passionate about a cause and want to do more than just write out a check to a major organization once a year, perhaps you should consider converting that passion into a new career. There are five main types of nonprofit businesses: trade associations, charitable organizations, social clubs, governmental groups (such as city, county, state, and federal agencies), and political groups (typically organized to promote certain policies, issues, or candidates).

In this chapter, we'll specifically be looking at charitable organizations, which must have a demonstrably benevolent component. Included are religious groups, museums, environmental and educational organizations, libraries, and many charity-type groups. They are also referred to as 501(c)(3) organizations, because that is the number of the IRS Code under which they are described.

What Does "Nonprofit" Really Mean?

The main distinction between a nonprofit and for-profit organization is how the profits are used. Note: Both types of organizations must make a profit to survive; the difference is that in the case of nonprofits, the profits are redistributed for the advancement of the company, rather than as income to the owners.

In addition to forgoing the profits, you also need to be able to forgo control of the company. Typically, nonprofits are organized so that the board, not an individual, has control over matters such as salaries, benefits, employment, and general policy. In fact, you will even need to excuse yourself from the vote on matters affecting your employment. In other words, the cause you are supporting must truly come first.

Reasons to Start Your Own

Is starting a new nonprofit organization really the best way to accomplish the goals you have in mind? Other alternatives, including collaborating with or working for an existing nonprofit, establishing an informal club or association (a good idea for groups with annual budgets under $25,000), or forming a for-profit business, may prove a quicker, more efficient way to achieve your goals and result in the best benefit to your target audience. That said, there are many reasons people might choose to start their own nonprofit.

You're the Only Game in Town

The first could be geographic: You may really be a believer in the policy work done by the Humane Society of the United States but don't live near their Washington, D.C., headquarters. In this instance, you could set up a nonprofit that fulfills a similar need in your community.

The Competition Is Tough

Another reason is the limited availability of nonprofit jobs in general. These jobs are usually highly competitive despite their often poor salaries. This is because they tend to attract two populations: young, idealistic workers straight out of college and older workers willing to sacrifice salary for personal fulfillment and benefits. You may have a strong desire to participate in conservation work, but none of the nearby organizations is hiring, or you don't match what they are looking for in an employee.

You'll Meet a Specific Need

A third reason (and possibly the best one) is that there currently isn't an organization already operating that is serving the need you're aiming to fill.

For example, your local area may not have:

- A no-kill rescue (either breed-specific or general)
- An educational foundation for a specific subject matter
- An educational foundation for a specific subset of the population
- A foundation for local artists
- An aid organization for specific professions (firemen, police, military, etc.)
- A charity foundation for the poor or homeless
- A victim-support organization
- . . . and limitless other ideas

Benefits of the Nonprofit Sector

Whether you choose to work for an existing nonprofit or start your own, it's important to know what the benefits are of operating as a nonprofit organization.

Taxes

If you qualify for nonprofit status, you'll pay no federal, state, or local taxes and will be able to devote a larger proportion of your resources to achieving your goals.

Other benefits include tax-exempt status on purchases (which you have to file for) and tax-deductibility of contributions you receive. If you're running a nonprofit environmental travel company, for instance, you can use the fact that your program fees are tax deductible as a selling point.

Employee Benefits

Also, for tax reasons, it's easier for nonprofit organizations to reward employees with fringe benefits rather than fat salaries. Benefits packages at nonprofit organizations often include generous vacation time and sick pay, low premiums on medical and dental insurance, good retirement plans, tuition reimbursement, and often flexible work schedules without significant overtime.

The ABCs of 501(c)(3)s

According to the Society of Nonprofit Organizations (SNPO), there are seven basic steps to starting your own nonprofit. (This organization maintains an excellent website, and it would be a great idea to make your very first step joining this organization.)

Step One: The Mission

First, you should define your organization's purpose and form, and write a mission statement. It should clearly explain why people will want to invest in your organization (as donors, volunteers, or recipients of service). Visit a few of your favorite nonprofits' websites to see some examples. They should be very easy to find and easy to understand.

Step Two: Form Your Board

In order to incorporate, you will be required to have a board of directors.

The SNPO has a publication for this process, accessible to its members. Note that the board of directors will be in charge of everything about the organization, from policy to payroll. Be sure you choose people you trust; this is possibly the most important decision you'll make.

Step Three: File Articles of Incorporation

This is necessary so that it establishes your company as a separate legal organization. This allows the company to have its own property and its own bank account, enables it to continue on after your passing, and last but not least protects you personally from liability. Nonprofit incorporation involves filing articles of incorporation (or other charter documents) with the appropriate local state office.

Step Four: Establish Rules

Write your organization's by-laws, or the rules you will adhere to. There are multiple guides on how to write by-laws. Visit the companion website for the best ones (go to *www.unplugyourhead.com/dowhatyoulove* for more info).

Steps Five and Six: Apply for Nonprofit Status

Attaining nonprofit status is actually a two-part process. First, apply with the IRS. (Ask your local IRS office for IRS publication 557 and IRS form 1023).

Next, after you have received your letter of determination from the IRS, apply for nonprofit status to your state department of revenue and your state department in charge of regulations.

Step Seven: Register

Lastly, register your organization with the state. Contact the Secretary of State (Corporate Division) and Attorney General (Charities Division).

Other Good Ideas

Other wise moves include applying for a solicitation license from your city (required by some cities before you can solicit funds.) You should also apply for sales tax exemption from your state and a nonprofit bulk-mail permit from your post office.

Obtain liability insurance, including Directors' and Officers' (or D & O) insurance. This type of insurance is necessary to protect your board members' assets.

Applying for Grants and Other Funding

Most nonprofits rely extensively on fundraising from private individuals and on grants. To be successful, you should structure your company so that you are able to tap a broad variety of funding sources.

While the preceding steps can take a very long time to see through to completion, it's important that you do not accept any money whatsoever until your letter of incorporation as a nonprofit comes through. Otherwise, you're personally liable for what you do with donated money. If you were later sued, it could wipe out your personal assets.

PITFALLS AND PERILS Once you jump through all of the hoops required to achieve nonprofit status, you'll need to make sure you don't do anything to jeopardize your exempt status. Following are some common traps you'll need to avoid.

Although you can pay reasonable salaries to yourself and the staff, you also need to be careful about how much money you can actually take in, regardless of profit. Specifically, you need to be careful to avoid "inurement." This term prohibits nonprofits from allowing any of its income to be paid to or property sold (below fair market price) to insiders such as officers, directors, or employees. This is an "absolute" requirement, meaning that any such payment or sale will allow the IRS to strip your exempt status.

A second pitfall is ensuring you don't generate too much unrelated business income (UBI). Basically, your organization may not receive regularly generated income from a trade or business that is not related to your mission. If you generate funds from a business activity but it is not regular, you will probably have to pay taxes on that income but it won't jeopardize your tax-exempt status (i.e., selling T-shirts at an annual fair).

If your organization earns more than $1,000 of such income during the year, it must file IRS form 990-T, Exempt Organization Business Income Tax Return. Too much UBI can threaten your tax-exempt status. You could also imperil your status if UBI activities require more time and attention than your mission.

Another potential minefield is lobbying. A 501(c)(3) organization has to be very careful if it engages in lobbying. Although some lobbying is permitted under certain circumstances, this is a very murky area. Encouraging anyone to support, propose, or oppose legislation could result in the loss of your exempt status, and may result in a fine as well.

A related stipulation is in regard to political campaigns. A 501(c)(3) organization cannot endorse or oppose any candidate for public office, nor can it make contributions to a political campaign, or even public statements for or against a candidate. This is another absolute prohibition, resulting in stripping the 501(c)(3) of its tax-exempt status.

Your organization may invite a political candidate to speak at an event only if there is no fundraising, the opportunity to speak is extended to other candidates seeking the same office, and if you do not indicate your support for or opposition to any candidate.

The best way to prevent losing your tax-exempt status is to focus on your mission—the reason your organization was founded—and make sure that all of your activities revolve around that purpose. ●

SUCCESS STORY

The pivotal moment in Beth Carrigan's life occurred when she was just five years old. Standing with her mother at a bus stop, she saw an elderly woman sitting by herself. Worried that the woman might be lonely, young Beth asked her mom, "Where is she going?" Her mother's answer would have a lifelong impact: "Why don't you go ask her?" She did. The resulting interaction planted the seeds for Beth's ongoing fascination with America's elders, and her future work with the Light Heart Foundation.

After a successful seventeen-year career in mortgage banking, Beth was ready for something more meaningful in her life. The decision was prompted by both of her parents becoming seriously ill, along with six other family members. She spent a lot of time in nursing homes and assisted-care facilities, and soon found herself visiting with the other people there, not just her family members. She discovered that many of the people "had delicious stories to share!" However, according to Beth, the average aide has just seventeen minutes per day per resident.

"Many times, the staff didn't know someone might have been a concert pianist."

Harold was one such resident. "He was sitting in the lobby of the retirement home. As I walked by he said, 'Hello you gorgeous thing. Come sit next to me! I have to tell you stories.'" She did, and soon discovered that despite being blind, Harold was a writer. At seventy-eight, he'd written lots of books, and he was currently using a machine to write. It was a laborious process, taking four hours to write one paragraph. Beth made a trip to Circuit City and purchased Harold a special tape recorder. Since he'd lost sensitivity in his fingers, he wasn't able to read Braille, so she used Velcro to make buttons for the recorder that he could feel. She also bought him lots of ninety-minute tapes.

Before they went to dinner that night, he called his publisher and said he was working on his next book. "He was very excited," Beth shares. Harold died four days later, thinking his next book would be published and his legacy passed on to his children.

Sadly, it's been estimated that more than half of all nursing home patients don't have visitors. Beth decided to set up a foundation dedicated to reaching out to the elderly and fostering intergenerational learning and exchange. "Our senior population has value. They have stories to share." The Light Heart Foundation was born. Her first task was to find and train volunteers, and teach them how to talk to the elderly. "I didn't just want a project or a visit. I wanted to build some intentional relationships. These places don't have to be miserable."

Beth faced a lot of challenges in setting up the foundation. "There were many Catch-22 situations. You can't qualify for many grants from a home office, but renting an office is expensive." Similarly, many of the grant applications asked, "What have you done that's noteworthy?" As a result, a lot of money came from her own pocket, as well as endless fundraising drives. "I'd open an envelope and find one dollar, but that was fabulous! Every dollar counts."

Today, the Light Heart Foundation is involved in several community projects connecting the elderly to their communities. Project HUG (Helping Unite Generations) is a program that connects children (K-12) with seniors in their communities. "It makes a difference in the lives of 10,000 people," says Beth.

Despite the program's success, there's still plenty of room to grow. The U.S. Census Bureau estimates that every day this year, 7,900 people will be turning sixty years old. By 2030, persons aged sixty-five or older will comprise 20 percent of the total U.S. population, more than twice their number in 2000. Beth and her foundation plan to greet this wave with "intelligence, responsibility, and joy!" You can learn more about Beth at *www.lightheartfoundation.org.* ●

Now, let's examine the concepts we've looked at in this chapter to see if right now, you feel starting your own nonprofit is "worth it" to you. You may find it helpful to write down your thoughts in a notebook or to discuss these issues with your friends or family. As you answer each question, try to think of specific instances to support your opinion.

Checklist | Is It Worth It?
How many of these statements do you agree with?

○ My proposed organization serves a specific, currently underserved need.

○ My passion for my cause is strong enough to endure a sea of red tape when getting started.

○ I'm willing to put my cause ahead of my salary and all other issues that affect me directly.

○ I understand that nonprofits exist primarily on donations, and I am comfortable with the idea of spending a significant amount of time fundraising.

If there are any statements you don't agree with, now is the time to carefully analyze the reasons why and determine how much of a roadblock this item represents in your overall plan.

SUMMARY OPERATING A NONPROFIT IS RIGHT FOR ME BECAUSE:

- I have a strong passion that I would love to dedicate myself to full-time.
- There is a demonstrable need for the service I want to offer.
- I have a good network to help pave the way.
- I'm not interested in just another job: I want to leave a legacy.

CHAPTER 12

Becoming a Caregiver

Are you one of the millions of Americans who is raising a child while also caring for a parent? Or perhaps you find yourself in a position of trying to care for your loved ones from a long distance. Often, these family obligations clash not just with each other, but also with the pressures of having to maintain full-time jobs. If you're caught up in a situation where you'd like to care for, or be more involved with the care of, your children, grandchildren, or elderly parents, you could consider a career switch to full-time caregiving. This choice makes it possible for you to be proactively involved in the care of the ones you love without having to balance external career demands. (Caution: This is only true if you choose to operate a formal center as outlined below, not if you apply for government funds for one-on-one care. In the latter case, you will not be eligible for funding.)

Naturally, personal caregiving is also an excellent choice for those without these types of family obligations if they have a strong desire to help others. An obvious caveat is that regardless of your personal situation, this type of career requires a particular personality type; caregivers must be dedicated, emotionally resilient, energetic, and patient.

Operating a Day Care Center

There are two types of day care centers: franchises and home-based operations. Regardless of which type you choose, you'll be dealing with a lot of regulations: municipality, county, and state laws, as well as federal recommendations. You will need to be licensed, and expect to be audited by state social workers to ensure you're in compliance with age-specific guidelines for each child under your care.

Franchises

The easiest (but costliest) option is to purchase a franchise. There are dozens of options available, requiring anywhere from $30,000 to over $1 million of liquid capital. The benefits of purchasing a franchise over starting a day care center from scratch include: name recognition (which can be an important consideration for parents when choosing where to place their child); the potential for a more significant income; and best of all, having the legal, licensing, and other business aspects already worked out for you.

Home-Based Businesses

On the other hand, you may prefer the idea of operating a small day care out of your home, especially if you'd like to be there for your own children. Home-based operations are usually not very lucrative, but they can provide you with the satisfaction of remaining home with your child or grandchild while earning what will likely amount to a part-time salary. If you choose this path, there are many factors you'll need to consider, such as minimum space requirements (both indoor and outdoor) per child.

Prior to receiving your license, your home will need to be child-proofed in order to pass inspection. For example, you'll need safety latches on all cabinets, and potential hazards such as wood stoves and swimming pools will need to be properly secured. Play areas must be flat and free of hazards. Wherever the laws aren't in agreement (i.e., county and state), follow the strictest one.

Ramp Up Your Knowledge

Whether you choose to operate a home-based day care center or a franchise, it would be a good idea to enroll in a few early childhood development courses at your local community college. This will not only help you provide better care for your charges, but will also keep you abreast of issues that are of concern to state legislators and social workers. It can also help make your business more competitive.

Other Child Care Options

If you don't have a family of your own to care for, you might also consider caregiving options outside the home.

Nannies . . . and Mannies!

One such option is to work as a nanny for an individual family. Nannies can be part-time or full-time; live-in, or live-out. Live-in nannies are often provided their own quarters and a family car to run errands and transport the children. Full-time nannies can also be live-out, in which case you'll spend your evenings at your own home and drive your own vehicle. Both types of full-time nannies can expect to have weekends and holidays off, as well as an extensive paid annual vacation (sometimes one month or more). Nannies for wealthy families sometimes get to accompany the family on trips, both domestic and overseas. Finally, some nannies (usually those working through agencies) report receiving hospitalization coverage and workmen's compensation, as well as other benefits.

You can take nanny courses at your local college or attend specialized schools such as the National Academy of Nannies in Colorado or Northwest Nannies, Inc. (which is also a placement agency). Those who have undergone such training can expect significantly higher salaries, as much as $800 per week.

Lest you think that being a nanny is a career choice restricted to women, *The Today Show* recently ran a feature on "mannies," or men who enter the nanny profession. Of the 600,000 nannies working today, most are female, but there are many reasons a family might prefer a male nanny. For one thing, there is an element of increased security in having a male presence looking after children. Second, families with small boys might prefer a male who will toss the football with them for forty-five minutes or might even get involved in coaching their school sports. Third, single women raising boys might be seeking a stable male presence in their lives (not to mention someone with handyman skills!).

Newborn Care

Another career with a growing demand is newborn caregiving. Thanks to the Family Medical Leave Act, more and more fathers are taking an active role in the care of their newborn children. Despite the increased ability to have both spouses at home, working couples today still need assistance, especially if they have other children at home. It's not uncommon for extended family (grandparents, aunts, etc.) to either live in other states or to have full-time jobs of their own. Newborn caregivers provide the family with advice and guidance on caring for newborns, plus an additional presence so that the new parents can give their time and attention to the other children or to running the household. Some pediatric nurses make a very profitable living by moving into homes with newborns for the first two weeks to a month, helping the families ease into their new routine.

Working with Aging Seniors

Day care centers and personal caregiving (such as nannies) are not only for children. Many adults have older parents who, while not infirm or mentally incapacitated enough to warrant being in a nursing home, still require some daytime supervision while the adult child is at work. Whether it's offering simple companionship or personal services, there is a growing segment of the population who find themselves in need of a senior caregiver.

A Growing Need

According to the Census Bureau, by 2010, one in five Americans will be aged sixty-five or older. Currently, one in four households is engaged in some form of unpaid caregiving for senior family members. Many of these families find themselves struggling to handle the stresses of providing care while also working full-time. Alternatively, some families have made the decision to forgo one spouse's income in order to provide this care, but then face increased financial pressure from operating on one income. That said, it's clear why *Entrepreneur* magazine ranks senior day care centers as one of the top ten growing businesses.

Medical Careers

Senior caregiving can be either medical or nonmedical in nature. Medical caregiving includes the work of licensed practical nurses (LPNs) or physician assistants. This work is most often found in nursing homes. These careers require more extensive training than nonmedical options, but it can often be attained at your local community college.

Nonmedical Careers

Nonmedical care can include everything from assistance preparing hot, nutritious meals, the chance to run errands, going grocery shopping, or providing transportation to doctor appointments. As with childcare, you can work for one specific family or operate a center. These centers also provide a place where older adults living at home can enjoy social activities and interact with their peers, necessary elements of dignity and self-worth. Operating a senior day care center could allow you the opportunity to keep your own watchful eye over an aging parent while providing a service for others in need.

As with child care, senior care involves licensing and regulation at the local, county, and state levels. Whether or not you're purchasing a franchise, you'll need to ensure you have adequate legal and financial counsel from the outset.

Working with the Ill or Disabled

A third segment of the population requiring caregivers are the severely ill or disabled. For many of these individuals, having just a few hours of home care each day can mean the difference between being forced into a nursing home and living an independent life.

New Job Creation

Thanks to the efforts of an organization known as ADAPT (American Disabled for Attendant Programs Today), the Bush administration signed a law in 2006 that provides $2 billion in state funding to help move such individuals out of nursing homes and into their own homes. This money is just a drop in the bucket compared to what the government currently spends on nursing homes, and as it turns out, home care is much more cost-effective on a per person basis than institutionalization. That said, there is a growing movement—backed by federal government support—to allow the ill and disabled to live better, more independent lives. This will ultimately translate into a growing market for caregivers as well. The program is projected to help 100,000 people in thirty states to move out of nursing homes by 2011.

PITFALLS AND PERILS No matter which branch of caregiving you decide to pursue (children, the elderly, or the disabled), it's likely you'll have to undergo an intense screening process: background and credit checks, criminal history, and sometimes even drug testing. The truth is, you should also be performing the same examination of those you'll be caring for, especially if you'll be working in someone else's home.

These days, it's fairly easy to find out if someone is a registered sex offender, if they've filed for bankruptcy, if criminal charges have been filed against them, or if they've participated in a lawsuit. In today's litigious society, it's a good idea to find out if a potential client has a history of suing previous providers. You can start with Google searches and work your way to paid background reports (available for a fee from many websites). It's also perfectly acceptable to ask potential clients for references. When you obtain them, be sure to follow up with a phone call.

Most of all, trust your instincts. This is especially important when working in as sensitive an industry as personal caregiving. If either the client or a member of his family gives you a sense of something being awry, you should refuse to work in their home and seek another assignment.

The same goes for anyone you employ to look after your clients. If you are running a day care center of some type, it's highly likely that you won't be doing so alone. The news is full of stories of people at such centers who have abused those they were caring for. Be extra careful when selecting your staff.

If you will be acting as a solo caregiver for someone in your family, there are several common pitfalls you need to be aware of. First, it's not uncommon for caregivers to be so dedicated to their charges that they neglect their own health and well-being. This will lead to burnout, affecting you and your charge in the long run. It's important to factor in vacations and short-term breaks so that you can recharge your own batteries.

A second pitfall is that caregivers are frequently so busy that they don't have time to track down resources that could greatly simplify their lives (i.e., caregiver support groups, networks, car pool programs, etc.). It's a classic Catch-22 that is best resolved by doing a full investigation of these services before you enter caregiving full-time.

Finally, caregivers can become so isolated with their care receiver that they lose touch with the outside world. This can lead to depression and have other negative long-term effects. ●

SUCCESS STORY

At age fifty-nine, Felicia was divorced and her children grown. Despite working full-time for an electronics firm, she still spent at least five hours of each day with her parents, who were both in their eighties. Her father has Parkinson's, which is slowly progressing. Her mother is in otherwise good health, but tires easily. Felicia and her sister explored assisted-living facilities, but their parents really wanted to stay in their own home. They tried paying an outside caregiver to care for them, but this too was rejected after a short while.

"Listen," her dad told Felicia one day. "Why don't we just pay you to care for us until we're gone?" At first, Felicia balked at the notion of taking her parents' money, but there was no way she could afford to quit her job to care for them. The decision became easier after her father had to be admitted to a nursing home for recuperation after a hospital stay, where he eventually developed bedsores. "It became obvious to me that he wasn't getting the right care."

After talking it over with her sister, Felicia and her parents went to a lawyer to draw up a personal care contract. In exchange for a lump sum of money that would allow Felicia to quit her job, Felicia committed to taking care of both of her parents in their own home, for as long as possible. She also consulted with an accountant, who advised her about the tax ramifications (she had to pay state and federal taxes, as well as FICA and Medicare on this income).

Overall, Felicia's happy to have made the change. She and her sister no longer feel guilty for having to hire someone else to be there for her parents, and her parents are happy to remain in their own home. Strange as it may seem, Felicia also has more time for herself. Before, she was dividing her time between a full-time job, five or more hours each day visiting her parents, and maintaining her own household. Today, she lives and works in her parents' home, providing her with peace of mind about their care, a more structured schedule, and some time to herself. She has networked with other caregivers in the area, and they have worked out a schedule to provide each other with some much-needed respite by combining activities (carpooling for doctor's appointments and grocery shopping, etc.).

Her sister is also pitching in. Although she lives in another state, she comes to visit twice a year for one-week stays. Felicia uses the opportunity to visit her grown kids and "be taken care of for a change." With each passing year, the work gets more tiring and challenging. That said, she has no regrets. "I can't put a price on my parents' happiness," Felicia says. ●

Now, let's examine the concepts we've looked at in this chapter to see if right now, you feel a career in caregiving is "worth it" to you. You may find it helpful to write down your thoughts in a notebook or to discuss these issues with your friends or family. As you answer each question, try to think of specific instances to support your opinion.

Checklist | Is It Worth It?
How many of these statements do you agree with?

○ I understand that caregiving, while rewarding, is also intensely draining, both physically and emotionally.

○ I am willing to invest time researching the various local, state, and federal regulations regarding caregiving, and modify my home if necessary.

○ I am prepared to research all available avenues of support. I understand that I don't have to do it all myself.

○ I understand the importance of trusting my instincts when it comes to potential clients and employees, and I am willing to conduct due-diligence for both.

If there are any statements you don't agree with, now is the time to carefully analyze the reasons why and determine how much of a roadblock this item represents in your overall plan.

SUMMARY CAREGIVING IS PERFECT FOR ME BECAUSE:

- Providing quality care to a loved one (or someone else's loved one) is personally satisfying.
- I have a tremendous amount of physical and emotional stamina.
- Money is not my main motivator. You can't put a price on making a difference in someone's life, every single day.
- There are many resources available to caregivers, and I plan to research and make good use of them.

CHAPTER 13

Changing Your Job, Not Your Career

Maybe you are among that rare breed of professionals: someone who has already been doing what you love for a long time, perhaps even from the inception of your professional career. You honestly can't picture yourself doing anything else and yet. . . .

Mondays are no longer a day you look forward to, you come home tired and frustrated, and more than ever, you're looking forward to a retirement that's not necessarily around the corner. Even if it were possible to stop working tomorrow, you don't have another avocation calling you to which you'd rather be dedicating your time.

In cases such as these, it may not be that you need to completely retool your career. Maybe all you really need is a different environment. The good news for you is that unlike most of the people reading this book, you probably won't need to invest in a significant amount of secondary education, balance two careers as you transition from one to the next, or subject yourself and your family to a major transformation. Well, at least not all three. One of these could still apply, depending on circumstances.

Switching Industries but Not Your Field

Maybe the nature of what you do is really in your blood. For instance, you could really be a numbers guy, always calculating costs and benefits—even for one brand of toothpaste over another. As the years pass, however, you're growing tired of doing profit analysis for your corporate clients at Ernst and Young. You know that you're good at what you do, but the professional challenge isn't there anymore. Frankly, you don't have much invested in the success or failure of your clients other than a responsibility to ensure that you do your own job accurately.

Same Work, More Meaning

Most people with professional backgrounds in accounting, finance, economics, marketing, and management can experience a huge increase in personal fulfillment by switching industries, such as from a corporate setting to a nonprofit or local government. A CPA may not care about the millions of dollars she is managing for a *Fortune* 500 company; they are likely just numbers on an Excel spreadsheet. This could change drastically when she applies the same skills in a job for her local town, managing funds for roads she drives on every day. Alternatively, she could go to work for a national or international charity, where she can relate the numbers she works with to lives saved or houses built.

Those with degrees in law or medicine can do the same. It's not uncommon for doctors with experience in cosmetic surgery, for instance, to shift gears and specialize in reconstructive surgery for victims of fires, wars, or abuse. ER nurses can shift to private nursing, small medical practices, or nursing homes. Obstetricians may switch to reproductive oncology. In the field of law, criminal prosecutors may shift to defense, or vice versa.

Training the Next Generation

Professionals may also choose to stop practicing in their field but stay involved in it by becoming a teacher. Opportunities exist for teaching young people as well as in adult education. (There is an entire chapter devoted to this topic, Chapter 14.)

Fewer Costs, All the Benefits

The beauty of changing industries is that most of the time, your skills, background, and experience are all 100 percent transferable to your new setting. Sometimes, there may be additional training or certifications involved, but nothing like the additional training you would face when starting a new career from scratch. There is also likely to be zero transition time: you just need to get your resume in good shape and actively look for a new job.

Of course, it's also possible that your new job may involve a change in location or compensation, so you'll have to weigh these consequences against the increase in fulfillment you'll achieve in your new setting. As the old MasterCard commercial might have put it: "Price of moving 10,000 miles to work in a better job: $8,000. Waking up with a smile on Mondays: priceless."

Firing Your Boss and Working for Yourself

Maybe it's not the corporate environment you find unfulfilling, but having to report to a nine-to-five job for someone else—anyone else. Perhaps you're one of those people who loses an hour each way, each day in your commute. Or you'd like to be able to take time out of the middle of your day to spend time with your grandchildren. Or you and your spouse have a new outdoor hobby and don't want to be limited to enjoying it only on the weekends. The reasons for wanting to break free of a nine-to-five schedule are as diverse as the people wanting to make a change.

If this sounds like you, you could consider continuing to work in your chosen profession, but to do so as a consultant, independent contractor, or private business owner. To clarify the terms, a consultant is someone who offers the same service to multiple companies, though not necessarily at the same time. An independent contractor is someone who works on a part-time or limited basis for one employer, but files his own taxes and does not receive benefits. A private business owner is someone who operates the business for which they work.

All three of these options can provide you with a much more flexible schedule, but be prepared for an initial period where you may end up working longer and harder in order to get your business established or find clients.

Independent Contractors

Of the three, the easiest transition may be to independent contractor status. Perhaps you have benefits under your spouse's job or social security, or are able to secure private health care. You like your job, generally speaking, but would like to work fewer hours or a more flexible schedule. Depending on the size of your company, how long you've worked there, and the nature of your work product, you may be able to approach your boss with a proposal to provide the same services you're currently providing, but as an independent contractor. Due to the fact that they will no longer need to pay your benefits (which can be expensive), your company may actually find this option appealing.

Often, companies that don't already offer flextime or telecommute options may prove resistant to the notion of working out such a schedule for you—as an employee. A common complaint is "if we do this for you, we'd have to allow everyone the option to telecommute/work flexible hours, etc." But if you're not an employee, this is no longer true.

Naturally, it's important to give careful consideration to offering this suggestion to your boss. It does have the potential to backfire; management may feel that you no longer have a vested interest in your employment with the company and could decide to let you go. That said, if you've been a hard working and productive employee and can phrase your request in a professional and meaningful manner, there's a good chance your company might go for it.

Consulting Versus Launching a Business

Working as a consultant means offering your services to one or more companies. It's very similar to the third option, operating your own business, although not entirely. Consultants can file taxes as individuals, don't need to incorporate, and can take on a variety of tasks without having to outline a specific product line.

Owning your own company is much more complex and requires much more thought and organization. Consultancy is ideal if you're operating as a one-person business and have a handful of regular clients who will be your main sources of income.

PITFALLS AND PERILS A proper discussion of the merits and downfalls of going into business for oneself would require an entire book, rather than one section of one chapter of a book. So, make sure you read the books suggested in the Online Resources Appendix under "Self-Employment" (*www.unplugyour head.com/dowhatyoulove*) if this is an option you are considering. That said, here are a few things you should be aware of, that apply to all three categories.

First, in all three of these situations, the tax burden (collection and payment) is going to shift to you. The only time this won't be true is if you work as an independent contractor exclusively for one company (or alternatively, a placement agency such as Robert Half). In that case, the employing company will still issue you a W2. If you're working as a consultant or business owner, you should report your income and pay quarterly taxes to the IRS.

Even if you're primarily planning to operate as a consultant, you should at least file for an employer identification number to file your business taxes. This way, you'll be able to keep your personal assets somewhat protected, although they won't be as protected as they would if you set yourself up as a small corporation (S-Corp).

The choice of setting up as an S corporation, limited liability company (LLC), or other structure is complicated. You can get free assistance from the Small Business Administration. The IRS also has some online guidelines.

Second, you'll need to meet with an accountant to discuss the types of tax deductions that you can legitimately take (home office deductions, mileage, etc.). Most people have at least some false assumptions they believe are accurate . . . until that auditor from the IRS shows up at their door!

Third, as Larry's story will illustrate, when you're operating a business with a spouse, friend, or other partner, it's important to outline and discuss each person's expectations regarding who is in charge of the business. The closer the relationship, the more important the discussion.

Fourth, you need to be aware that working for yourself can be much more difficult in many ways than reporting to a job—even a job you don't like. There are numerous factors that go on behind the scenes in keeping a business solvent, and you will need to familiarize yourself with all of them.

Since no one will care about the success of your business more than you will, don't be surprised to initially find yourself working long hours and through weekends and holidays to keep things going. That said, it's important to decide early on exactly which responsibilities you'll be taking on and what you can afford to delegate. Most small business owners wish they had delegated more to someone else, earlier in the process. It would be wise to economize on glitz and flash in order to afford the services of a bookkeeper, accountant, personal assistant, etc. Your health and sanity are possibly your most precious assets, after all.

Speaking of your health, when making this type of shift it's important to understand the impact your new employment status will have on your existing health coverage. Will you be able to afford private health insurance? Since virtually all private health care policies include pre-existing condition clauses, you'll need to decide if you want to get screened and treated for certain conditions now at a lower dollar cost, or face the possibility of policy exclusions later. ●

SUCCESS STORY

Immediately after attaining his business degree with a specialization in accounting, Larry landed a great job working for the State of Arizona Office of the Auditor General. After three years in state government, he switched industries to the corporate sector, starting with a job in financial and strategic planning for the electronics giant Sperry Corporation.

As the years progressed, Larry's career blossomed and expanded. He moved from controller for a securities and investment broker to controller for real estate investment company. Finally, after twenty financially successful years in his profession, he and his wife, Mary, began considering how to make improvements in their quality of life.

"My wife is also a CPA, and I was tired of working at the mercy of someone else." The couple first looked for practices in the Phoenix area and came across a practice for sale in Prescott Valley (a small town about seventy miles north of Phoenix). A Phoenix native, Larry "hadn't really considered leaving Phoenix" prior to that point, since all of his friends and family were there. After analyzing the practice, however, it made good economic sense. The couple also had three young children at the time and thought living in the smaller town would be great place to raise them.

The practice the couple acquired had two partners—one wanted to move to Phoenix and the other wanted to retire. Since they bought an existing practice, they had a nice client base from which to build. "I would recommend buying an existing practice rather than starting from scratch since you have cash flow from the outset. It also gives you a nice base to build referrals."

Another positive step the couple took was to keep one of the previous partners working for them during tax season for the next three years. This helped in several ways. The clients weren't as apt to change accountants since the person they were familiar with was still there, and the new owners were able to use his wisdom, experience, and help during the time crunch of tax season. "It was a win-win-win for us, him, and our clients. Lots of times when practices are sold the new owner wants to do it all himself. If he can keep the prior owner involved it will help with client retention and be better in the long term," Larry shares.

As they made the change from desk jobs for separate companies to working together, the couple faced a few challenges. The main disadvantage of working together is that during tax season, both of them are busy. "When the children were younger it could put a stress on family life."

Larry recommends to anyone planning on working with a spouse: "One person needs to be in charge and this needs to be understood ahead of time. Otherwise you will be in a power struggle all of the time."

Transitioning from a corporate job to an individual tax-based practice also involved a shift to work that is seasonal rather than the same year-round. "The biggest challenge with a tax and accounting practice is the compression of the work in the first four months of the year. During the busyness of that time we would often run behind on the regular monthly work, so even after tax season there was a lot of catch-up time." As a result, the first few years found the couple very busy year-round.

"Once we were through the first few years and could afford to hire more staff, the workload compression decreased and the work became more satisfying," Larry says. The couple's initial investment has paid off with more free time in the off-season. "We are now able to work less and make more."

Larry stresses that you can't just go from starting your own business to enjoying the rewards overnight. "If you are going to start your own business, you need to learn all phases of the operation in the first few years before you can take time off." In their CPA work, Larry and Mary "see lots of businesses that think they only need to be there sometimes and that it will take care of itself. Unless you know all facets of the business, you will have some struggles and maybe not make it. So learn and understand everything."

The couple also suggests new business owners find experts they can rely on to improve the business. "You need to understand everything, but you don't need to *do* it all. Especially to the detriment of other activities and your personal life," Larry says. ●

If you are considering going into business for yourself, you should investigate joining an association such as NASE (National Association for the Self-Employed). These associations provide discounted health care policies, motor club benefits similar to AAA, travel discounts, legal assistance, and myriad other benefits, usually at a very reasonable monthly rate.

Now, let's examine the concepts we've looked at in this chapter to see if right now, you feel firing your boss is "worth it" to you. You may find it helpful to write down your thoughts in a notebook or to discuss these issues with your friends or family. As you answer each question, try to think of specific instances to support your opinion.

Checklist | Is It Worth It?

How many of these statements do you agree with?

○ I am willing to take the financial risks involved with being an independent contractor, consultant, or private business owner.

○ I understand that initially, I may have to work even harder and have even less free time in order to achieve greater flexibility later.

○ If we'll be working together, my spouse and I are willing to agree on a power structure for the business. The same is true for other potential business partners.

○ I understand the importance of obtaining good legal, financial, and tax advice before embarking on my solo journey.

○ I am confident that I will be able to obtain health insurance for myself and my family.

If there are any statements you don't agree with, now is the time to carefully analyze the reasons why and determine how much of a roadblock this item represents in your overall plan.

SUMMARY LEAVING MY JOB MIGHT SAVE MY CAREER BECAUSE:

- I already love what I do; I just don't love where I do it.
- Changing industries has the potential to reinvigorate my love of my career and my sense of fulfillment.
- I am ready to escape the expectations and limitations of working for someone else.
- Being responsible for my own success is worth the risks associated with leaving my full-time job.
- My spouse and family are ready to support me in this endeavor and understand that a few short-term sacrifices may be necessary.

CHAPTER 14

Teaching Others

Teaching is a popular choice for those pursuing second careers. After all, whatever your previous career choice was, someone had to teach it to you. You can now either pass the baton to future generations or work to prepare tomorrow's work force by teaching general education classes. There are also myriad opportunities for teaching adult learners: either life skills or enrichment courses.

Is Teaching Right for You?

Those who are considering a career in teaching—no matter what the level—should be sure they have the following personality traits: good listening skills, the ability to simply explain complex topics, good organizational skills, patience, and an undying enthusiasm for their subject matter. The best teachers are the ones who can inspire even reluctant learners to have an interest in their topic. If you feel you fit the profile, let's look at the options.

Grade School and High School

If you love kids and want to be part of shaping young minds for future success, you may consider teaching at the grade school or high school level. There are two approaches to getting started as a teacher at this level.

The Traditional Route

The first is the traditional route: pursuing a master's degree in education or a closely related field, then obtaining the appropriate local certifications (which vary widely for each state and county), and finally applying for full-time work. This path is best suited for those still young enough to take their time with this approach; if you're a recent college graduate or still in your twenties, this would be the way to do it.

The Back Door: Substituting

Then there is an alternate route: using your existing degree and background to gain a foothold in your local school system (usually by substituting), and only then focusing your efforts on obtaining the certifications. Many school systems are so desperate for substitute teachers that they will hire you on the spot as long as you promise to pursue certification at some point.

For those with no teaching experience, spending some time substitute teaching before pursuing your certifications isn't a bad idea. Many people believe they would enjoy teaching, only to later find themselves overwhelmed by the masses of paperwork, seemingly endless state and federal mandates, unruly kids, and having to deal with irate or difficult parents. School systems can also be very political, which some people find off-putting.

Of course, substitute teaching is also significantly more trying than a full-time teaching career. Depending on how your local school system operates, each assignment could find you called to a different school with little more than an hour's notice, facing a bunch of kids who are very definitely "out to get you." The pay is usually poor and there are no benefits. That said, it's a great way to determine if you truly want to pursue teaching as a full-time career.

Getting Certified

Private schools haven't been as traditionally stringent with their entry requirements, but this has been changing in recent years. While it is possible to obtain teaching jobs in private school systems without teaching certifications or credentials, these jobs often pay significantly less than their public school counterparts.

For those truly committed to teaching as a second career but who need some assistance with the costs of credentialing and certification, there are two noteworthy programs.

Teach for America

Teach for America is a nonprofit organization that is currently part of the AmeriCorps program (pending renewal). The program provides college graduates and professionals with training and placement services in exchange for a two-year commitment to teach in rural or otherwise underserved areas. Those who are selected for the teaching corps attend an intensive five-week summer institute that covers "teaching as leadership, instructional planning and delivery, classroom management and culture, learning theory, and literacy development." Participants teach summer classes under direct supervision, are observed and critiqued, and participate in curriculum and lesson-planning clinics.

As long as Teach for America remains part of AmeriCorps, members can take advantage of two major benefits. First, they are granted loan forbearance on qualified existing student loans during their two years of service. Second, corps members receive an education award of $4,725 at the end of each year of service (totaling $9,450 over the two years), which may be used toward future educational expenses or to repay qualified student loans. Other benefits include scholarships for 100 partner graduate schools and job placement with twenty private firms.

Troops to Teachers

Another interesting program is Troops to Teachers, a creation of the Defense Activity for Non-Traditional Education Support (DANTES). You may be eligible for this program if you are currently active duty, were honorably discharged, have served in the reserves, or are retired from the armed forces. Each of these categories has different stipulations, but you can quickly check your eligibility on the website. According to the organization's website, "In most states, Troops to Teachers does not train or certify teachers, but rather helps you to find and enter the programs that do. Then, if you are eligible, Troops to Teachers provides financial assistance in the form of stipends or bonuses. Becoming a teacher with the assistance of TTT needs to be viewed as three distinct processes occurring at the same time. Some individuals begin teaching before becoming fully certified."

Community Colleges Versus Universities

If you possess a master's degree in any field, chances are good that you can find a job teaching at your local community college or university. That said, while a master's degree is sufficient to teach as an adjunct at both types of schools, it's becoming increasingly difficult to find full-time work without a PhD. Unfortunately, adjunct salaries are notoriously low, and it's almost impossible to earn a living as an adjunct alone. Most people who are teaching as adjuncts are either just starting out, retirees who don't need income, or have full-time careers doing something else. If you really enjoy teaching at the college level, obtaining a PhD might be a wise decision. These days, there are many accredited schools offering either part-time or online PhD programs.

There is also a growing need for online instructors and facilitators at all levels. Online teaching can provide you with the chance to teach regardless of physical proximity to colleges, to work from home, and to earn higher incomes than traditional classroom adjuncts. That said, online teaching also can be far more time consuming, often requiring you to be present and active online at least every other day, if not every day.

Trade and Vocational Schools

Outside of academia, teaching opportunities exist for every career that requires a license. Usually, these careers are focused on procedural versus theoretical learning processes and are often structured to include some form of apprenticeship. No longer the domain of "blue collar" trades such as mechanics, vocational schools (or career colleges, as they are also known) cover a wide range of subject matters. Examples include real estate, insurance, cosmetology, retail, tourism, hospitality, funeral services, and massage therapy. There is also a growing subset of specializations in the medical field: health information management, pharmacy technicians, and medical and nursing assistant programs.

There will always be a need for traditional vocational training for professions such as mechanics (now known as "automotive service technicians"), electricians, welders, and hair stylists. In addition, the service professions such as police, fire, and emergency medical personnel all have their own certification programs.

Finally, there are also opportunities to teach other adults the skills they'll need for their own second careers. Courses like "Career Skills" (focusing on using tools such as PowerPoint, Excel, etc.) and "Small Business Entrepreneurship" are just two examples.

All of these programs can be found at career colleges and vocational schools, and increasingly, as part of the curriculum at community colleges.

Costs and Benefits of Obtaining an Advanced Degree

Unless you are aiming for a position as a college or university professor, chances are good that a master's degree will be more than adequate to prepare you for a career in education. If you do wish to pursue a doctorate, you need to be very careful about your choice of degree programs. Recently, several PhD programs in education have come under fire for being too easy. "Critics say the programs mostly provide financial rewards—for the universities that collect tuition and for educators who pick up a credential that helps them earn a higher salary and a 'doctor' title," according to a recent article in the *Washington Post*. That said, if you do choose to pursue a PhD program, be sure you research it carefully before making a significant investment in tuition.

PITFALLS AND PERILS No matter the grade level you plan on teaching, you should be prepared to deal with a great deal of bureaucracy. This is especially true for those in primary and secondary education, who are inundated with mandate after mandate, largely thanks to programs like No Child Left Behind.

There is also a lot of paperwork. Many teachers enjoy teaching, but hate grading and term papers. "I enjoy the lecturing and the interaction, but not the grading" admits one college adjunct. "It can be painful" (both in terms of how little the students have retained from the lectures and reading, and in how long it can take).

Surprisingly for some, disciplinary issues are not limited to primary and secondary school. "I've had adult students show up to class drunk, high, or feeling belligerent," says one economics instructor at a career college. She's also had to deal with outright plagiarism and being challenged by older students who feel that they have the right to assert themselves over her due to their age. "You have to be able to take, and keep, tight control of the class," she shares.

Dealing with parents of students can also present a challenge. Sometimes the kids are great, but then you have to deal with an irate parent who wants to know why their child didn't get straight As.

Primary and secondary school teachers also need to be on the lookout for abuse, sometimes finding themselves in situations where they are morally and ethically required to take action.

Finally, some college professors, after attaining their PhD and a full-time faculty job, find that they have to spend an inordinate amount of time pursuing grants and writing research papers, rather than teaching. "It's all about the prestige factor, personally and for your academic institution," shares one professor. Ironically, he advises: "If you love to teach, becoming a full-time professor is probably not the answer." Becoming a tenured professor is really about continuing your own learning process and having the time and resources to be able to explore topics of interest to you. Many times, the students are secondary. ●

SUCCESS STORY

If there were an award for career diversity, Kent M. would definitely be in the running. After attaining his graduate degree in communications with a specialization in theater in the 1970s, he tried to find a job as a high school drama teacher.

"Unfortunately, drama teacher jobs are really hard to get; you practically have to wait for someone to die." Undeterred, he figured he'd apply for a position teaching English instead. There were no openings there, either, but the school was looking for someone to substitute teach English for special education. "In those days, they just lumped everyone together: the 'emotionally and mentally handicapped' as they called them back then, plus Down's syndrome kids and autistics." All of these special-needs students were housed together in one building, which was segregated from everyone else. When Kent showed up again after the first day, the school administrators were impressed. "Would you be willing to come back?" "Of course," he answered. Thus began Kent's first exposure to special education, which lasted one and a half years.

By day, Kent was teaching special-education English, but by night, he was pursuing his first love—acting—at a local theater. When the opportunity presented itself to direct the theater full-time, he jumped at the chance. He'd spend the next fifteen years in this role.

Eventually, the need to support his wife and family led to a career as a professional writer for AT&T, working on advertising and marketing copy. The work was lucrative but personally unrewarding, so when he was ready to claim his pension from AT&T and move into his final career, there was no question about his choice. "I've spent the last several decades doing what I had to do; now I'm going to do what I want to do." Kent returned to special education.

While he pursued his BA in education, Kent approached the local school system about substitute teaching. After the first session, he was once again asked, "Are you willing to come back?" by anxious school administrators. It turns out that the school had been having a very difficult time retaining substitute teachers for their special-education courses. "Each classroom has an aide, and some of the subs would come in, sit down at the desk and read the paper, and the aides would do all of the work." When Kent came to the classroom, he really gave it his all, and the impressed aides reported back to management. "They offered me the opportunity to be their permanent substitute, and there's never been a dull moment!" Kent says.

For Kent, substituting is the perfect choice. "It meets all of your needs and you can step away when you need to." As far as the poor pay, he says, "Money is not the most important object in your last career. Enjoy your last career. A large paycheck also comes at the price of a large part of your soul." To keep himself motivated, Kent keeps a sign that one of his special ed classes made for him on his desk. It says,

*Thank you, we real
ly like you Mr. M.*

Kent can't help but smile every time he sees it. "In corporate America, no one says thank you. Your paycheck is your thank-you." ●

Other Opportunities

Teaching opportunities are by no means limited to the options we've discussed. Actually, the opportunities are nearly *un*limited: community centers, nursing homes, corporations, churches, towns, and libraries all offer periodic or regular courses for adult learners. Local museums, zoos, and parks all need docents. Keep your eyes open within your own community, and let it be known among your personal networks that you are looking for opportunities to share your skills.

If you want to travel, there are numerous opportunities for those willing to teach English abroad (especially in Asian countries), to become a lecturer on a cruise ship, or to teach for the Department of Defense or international schools.

Now, let's examine the concepts we've looked at in this chapter to see if right now, you feel converting your hobby to a career is "worth it" to you. You may find it helpful to write down your thoughts in a notebook or to discuss these issues with your friends or family. As you answer each question, try to think of specific instances to support your opinion.

Checklist | Is It Worth It?
How many of these statements do you agree with?

○ I am patient, a good listener, and a good communicator.

○ I understand that there is more to a career in teaching than instruction, including lots of paperwork, regulations, and mandates from all levels of government.

○ I am willing to pursue further formal education if warranted.

○ I understand that most adjunct and substitute teaching positions have poor pay structures.

○ Becoming a full-time college professor may actually mean less time spent teaching and more time conducting research and applying for grants.

○ Disciplinary problems can exist at any level, and I am prepared to deal with them.

If there are any statements you don't agree with, now is the time to carefully analyze the reasons why and determine how much of a roadblock this item represents in your overall plan.

SUMMARY TEACHING IS THE RIGHT CHOICE FOR ME BECAUSE:

- I am ready to pass the baton to future generations.
- The rewards of positively impacting a person's life through education far outweigh the challenges.
- I would be most fulfilled by a career that leaves a legacy of learning.
- Substitute teaching provides an excellent way to assess my true potential as a teacher and can provide a foot in the door prior to becoming certified.
- There are numerous programs, grants, and incentive programs for new teachers.
- Teaching can be a ticket to paid travel abroad through ESL programs, Department of Defense and international schools, and even stints on cruise ships.
- Opportunities to teach are virtually unlimited; local communities are rich with various opportunities to serve as an educator.

CHAPTER 15

The Speaking Circuit

If you love interacting with people, enjoy teaching, and are passionate about a specific topic, you should consider a career as a professional speaker. There are three basic roads you can take: a freelance subject matter expert, a motivational speaker, or a professional presenter (working for one specific company).

Subject Matter Experts

If you are an expert in a specific subject matter (i.e., travel, corporate reorganization, sales management, etc.) you can make a career out of educating others on the subject. The more specific the niche, the better. There is a lot of competition out there, so being able to narrow your focus can help you stand out. You can always expand your topic as necessary. This is a great niche for those who have authored books, especially of the nonfiction, how-to variety.

Motivational Speakers

Or perhaps you have a compelling personal story: surviving illness or a natural disaster, achieving professional success despite many odds, overcoming a phobia. In that case, you might consider becoming a motivational speaker. This arena too, is a bit crowded, but there are also multiple opportunities if you know where to look.

Professional Presenter

Finally, you can also use your speaking abilities to present for one specific company. Colleges, universities, and technical schools are one of the major employers in this category. There are also opportunities to present for financial-planning companies, travel companies, corporate-training companies, and companies providing B2B (business-to-business) benefits or products.

Practice Makes Perfect: Learning the Art

If you have a lot of experience giving presentations, great! If not, this is where you'll need to start.

Join Toastmasters

For those with no prior experience speaking, you should join a group such as Toastmasters, which specializes in preparing people to speak in front of others. Membership is inexpensive, a $20 new member fee and $27 biannually. You can find local clubs by visiting the national Toastmasters site. Many of the local clubs have memberships open to all; others may set their own specific criteria. Since the clubs can vary considerably in personality, tone, and objectives, you should visit more than one before joining. To join, simply ask the club officer for an application. The officer will forward your completed application and fees to the national headquarters.

Give It Away

Once you've attained a level of comfort with Toastmasters, you should start getting booked to speak in front of groups—for free, that is. Speaking for free necessarily precedes speaking for a fee. For one thing, you will likely need to build your resume and testimonials before a company or organization will pay you money to speak in front of their group. For another, nothing seasons a speaker like practice, practice, practice. The more you do it, the easier it gets. By speaking often, you'll develop a natural rhythm and cadence, and one that works with various crowds. You'll learn which jokes work and which ones don't. You'll develop effective icebreakers and learn how to read signals from the audience to determine how the speech is going.

Some speaking experts say you should deliver between 50 and 100 free speeches before taking your first paid engagement. Naturally this depends on your prior experience, your own comfort level, and the possibility that a paid engagement may arise before you've reached a specific magic number. You'll know when you're ready to enter the world of paid engagements.

Learn from the Best

Another piece of advice is to regularly attend as many speaking engagements by other people as you can. One way to do this is to volunteer (or work part-time) at a conference center. Another way is to rent, borrow from the library, or watch on YouTube as many live presentations by famous speakers as you can. Examples include Tony Robbins,

Jack Canfield, John Gray, and Ellen Kreidman. Watch, take notes, and try to find a way to emulate their techniques.

Ready, Set, Go!

Once you're ready to take the plunge, there are three additional steps before you can accept your first paid speaking engagement. These include assembling a package, defining your audience, and choosing your preferred delivery mechanism (corporate events versus public seminars).

Assembling Your Package

The package should include a good, professional headshot, one short and one long demo video, a topic list, and your testimonials. These days, having a simple website with this information on it is an absolute necessity, and it's a good idea to also create some hard-copy mini-packages, or brochures.

Your headshot should capture your personality, yet still retain a professional quality. A studio shot is a must. For ideas on compiling a good presentation demo, visit one of the websites listed in the Online Resource Appendix and click on their top speakers' pages. Finally, be sure you follow the advice in Chapter 9 on the importance of a establishing a professional presence, including a simple but well-done website.

Define Your Audience

In assembling your package, you'll need to decide who your audience is. Do you see yourself presenting to individuals or companies? One critical mistake new speakers make is to develop a list of topics geared to individuals (i.e., "How to attract the love of your life") when they are hoping to get corporate bookings. Make sure your topic list reflects your chosen audience.

Private Events or Public Seminars

Incidentally, your choice of audience will also make a big difference in the type of speaking career you will have. Those preferring to speak to audiences made up of individuals would do well to look into "public seminars," which can be a very lucrative—although far more entrepreneurial—avenue. You'll be in charge of everything: from finding a venue, publicizing the event, issuing invitations, lining up other speakers, etc.

Public seminars can be either technical or motivational in nature. Technical seminars (such as those offered to doctors, lawyers, salespeople, etc.) are easier to break into, assuming you have strong credentials in the area. Motivational seminars can also be successful for newcomers, but you must have an absolutely compelling story (and a book or other product doesn't hurt). Pairing up with one or two other speakers and offering a multispeaker seminar will increase your chances of attracting a good-size crowd.

It's not uncommon for individuals to pay upwards of $1,000 per person for a weekend seminar, as well as their own airfare and accommodations.

Making Connections and Getting Booked

As an English teacher once quipped at a graduation ceremony, "Contrary to popular belief, it's not who you know—it's whom." Semantics aside, connections, as always, are the name of the game. There are several things you can do immediately to get the ball rolling.

Make Use of Your E-mail Signature

First, develop your personal e-mail signature. Be sure it includes your title, "Jane Doe, Professional Speaker," a link to your website, and your contact information. This signature should be included on every e-mail you send out. Don't be surprised when a family member, friend, or acquaintance says, "I didn't know you were a speaker! Would you be willing to give a talk at . . ."

Get Connected

Second, add all of this information to your social networking sites, such as LinkedIn and Facebook. If you don't have a profile on these sites, create one today! The world of interpersonal connections has already migrated online, and these sites are powerful networking tools.

Join a Service

Third, join a speaker-matching service such as SpeakerMatch. These companies provide you with a professional-looking online presence, as well as the opportunity to hear about speaking engagements (paid and unpaid) that you might not otherwise learn about.

Teach a Class

Another opportunity is to offer adult education enrichment courses at your local community college. There is a large segment of the adult population interested in taking courses for fun and personal enrichment. Many times, local colleges have short (six to eight week) noncredit "courses" available on a wide variety of topics. Typically, you will be responsible for designing the course based around your level of expertise, and the school will advertise it and pay you (often based on the number of enrollees). You can also charge an additional materials fee if you want to sell your book or other product. This can be a great way to get started as a speaker in your local area and will help build confidence for eventually speaking in front of larger groups.

Take Your Show on the Road—or Ocean!

If you love to travel, there is also the opportunity to approach the cruise line industry. The major lines are always looking for enrichment speakers, and you can often arrange to sail for free in exchange for giving a talk. The more you can tailor your talk to the destination, the better. While you will not be paid for your services, this is another way to enlarge your audience base and to potentially sell your secondary product.

The Importance of a Book or Product

Having a book or other product will not only boost the income from your speaking career, but it can also add credibility and prestige to your status as an expert. Some speakers report making considerably more from their "secondary" products than from the speaking engagement itself.

Writing a Book

If you do choose to create a book, be aware that the publishing industry is difficult to penetrate. The disadvantages of taking the traditional publishing route are the length of time from inception to publication; the stiff competition from other authors; the small percentage of revenue from each unit; and the lack of control over production issues.

The advantages, of course, include not having to deal with production issues and costs, and the ability for your product to reach a worldwide market through established distribution channels.

Even authors who do get publishing contracts are expected to engage in a tremendous amount of marketing and promotion. If your goal is to put that time and energy into promoting your speaking career, it might make more sense to self-publish a book, booklet, or workbook. For one thing, you can start with small amounts and build it as the success of your speaking career grows. For another, you'll be able to capture a significantly higher proportion of the profits. These days, print-on-demand publishing can be quite affordable, and depending on your topic, it might be the option that makes the most sense. If your speaking platform grows to the point that you are nationally recognized, a book deal from a major publisher may follow at a later date.

Endless Product Options

Products include DVDs, audio CDs, workbooks, calendars, posters, software programs, reports, consulting sessions, and even promotional materials such as T-shirts, hats, and toys based on your topic. Screensavers and decks of cards (motivational or informational) are two increasingly popular options.

Another product you can sell is your time. Some people will be so inspired by your presentation that they will be willing to hire you for one-on-one coaching or consultation. For many speakers, income earned from coaching or private consultation far exceeds their income from speaking engagements and also provides a steadier revenue stream.

While there are many people out there calling themselves "coaches," a true coach will have either a background in counseling or relevant training by a coaching institute. If you don't have this background, you should bill yourself as a "consultant" instead.

Whether you bill yourself as a coach or a consultant, one thing is vital: Have a predetermined fee and service structure in place before you advertise your services. It's important to instill a sense of confidence in your abilities from the very beginning. It's also essential to capture testimonials from as many clients as possible. You'll need to get your initial testimonials from people (employers, past clients, etc.) who have worked with you in another capacity and who are willing to be quoted about your best attributes. "Jane provides a high level of customer service and care to each person she meets," etc.

PITFALLS AND PERILS Nothing can derail a successful career in public speaking as quickly as a bad performance. While it's natural to be somewhat nervous your first time in front of a group, by following the previous advice in this chapter (joining Toastmasters, giving countless free talks) you should be able to eliminate much of this nervousness.

On the other hand, the biggest blunders speakers make are borne of over-confidence. Lack of preparation for a particular speech, including researching the audience, is the number one mistake. Knowing and respecting your audience is very important. Everything from the types of jokes you can make, to the outfit you're wearing, to the tone of your talk (conversational or formal) can matter a great deal. Similarly, arriving late or going over your allotted time are signs of disrespect.

If you're planning on using visual aids (such as PowerPoint presentations), make sure you are comfortable with all of the equipment. Test it beforehand and have backups available. Also, be prepared to give your speech without these aids in case of a total technology failure (it happens more often that you might think). Visual aids should be there to break up the monotony of the presentation; they shouldn't form its backbone. You, your energy, and your interaction with the audience are what will drive the presentation forward, not your PowerPoint slides. Speaking of your visual aids, be sure that they are easy to read and not too crowded. Simplicity is king.

Another mistake some presenters make is to read their speeches. There is an excellent quotation on the speaker training website *http://presentations training.org*: "The last time somebody read to you, it was your mother, and she was trying to get you to fall asleep." More needn't be said.

Finally, every attendee at every speech you give should be given an evaluation form. (Be sure to check your ego at the door.) Evaluation forms not only provide you with a realistic assessment of how you're doing, but can also be fodder for new material. All evaluation forms should include questions such as "What didn't the speaker cover that you would have liked to have heard?" or "What did you like best/least about today's talk?" You can also use evaluation forms to promote a product: "I've handed out evaluation forms for every seat today. All those who turn in an evaluation form will be entered to win a free workbook." Also be sure you capture e-mail or snail mail addresses on these forms (on a voluntary basis) in order to stay in touch through your newsletter or other marketing materials. Last but not least, evaluation forms are a great way to capture testimonials. ●

SUCCESS STORY

Sunny Schlenger was introduced to the concept of professional organizing while attending graduate school for psychology. Right away, she realized she'd found a great match for her skills. When she was involved in a car accident a short while later, the long recovery period gave her a lot of time to think. "I knew that I wanted to focus on organizing as a career."

Sunny knew that to promote her business, she'd have to get out in front of groups. A naturally shy and introverted person, she immediately started out on the wrong foot. "I was too shy to attend a public speaking course," she confides. "So I taught myself public speaking from a book." That was a big mistake, she says.

She joined the local Rotary group, and was the only woman. Her first speaking engagement was a total disaster. "I went home and cried for three or four days." She was in her mid-twenties at this time.

Still, her passion for her topic kept her going, and she just kept "learning by doing." Eventually, the International Platform Society invited her to speak in front of a crowd of 1,000 people, and she realized that she'd come a long way.

Soon, Sunny realized the need for a book on her topic. Not only would a book aid her credibility for her speaking career, but there was also a genuine need for something new in the market. "Whenever I would visit clients, I would always notice lots of books on organizing on their shelves. Unfortunately, that's where they stayed—on the shelf." Sunny recognized the need for a book that clients would actually use. A few years later, she was afforded the opportunity to work with another author on just the right book, *How to Be Organized in Spite of Yourself.* The book became a Book of the Month Club selection.

With a book and a mounting track record of public speaking engagements, Sunny's career as a professional organizer and lifestyle coach grew as well. Today, Sunny runs a full-time coaching business for individuals who feel overloaded by the "stuff" of life. Her goal is to help clients experience a life that "feels whole, organized, and full of purpose." Sessions are created to support, guide, and encourage individuals to manage their hours and office space, daily hassles, and home environment to achieve success.

She has also taken the concept of organizing to the next level by integrating it with another of America's growing fascinations—spirituality. The result, *Organizing for the Spirit*, was published in 2004.

She has two pieces of advice for those thinking about a career in public speaking. "First, don't think you can teach yourself public speaking," she chuckles. Second, work hard on finding your own voice, whether writing or speaking. "It took me awhile to find a style that wasn't a corporate voice, the voice of my coauthor, or someone else's entirely. Once I found my own voice, my writing and speaking rose to another level."

Hundreds of paid speaking engagements later, Sunny shares that success is not a final destination. "You never stop growing and learning. You never 'get there,' because 'there' keeps moving." The more authentic and true to your goals you remain, the more your idea of perfection is shaped by your own personal growth. ●

Now, let's examine the concepts we've looked at in this chapter to see if right now, you feel launching a career as a professional speaker is "worth it" to you. You may find it helpful to write down your thoughts in a notebook or to discuss these issues with your friends or family. As you answer each question, try to think of specific instances to support your opinion.

Checklist | Is It Worth It?

How many of these statements do you agree with?

○ I understand that speaking well is an acquired skill. I am willing to take the appropriate courses to maximize my public speaking skills before embarking on this career path.

○ Practice makes perfect. I am willing to give 50 to 100 free speeches before expecting to be paid to give a talk.

○ I am willing to advertise myself as a product, and one that people can believe in.

○ I understand the necessity of having a secondary product, such as a book, workbook, CD, or private consulting service to supplement my income and add credibility to my status as an expert.

If there are any statements you don't agree with, now is the time to carefully analyze the reasons why and determine how much of a roadblock this item represents in your overall plan.

SUMMARY A CAREER IN PUBLIC SPEAKING IS PERFECT FOR ME BECAUSE:

- I have expertise in an uncommon area or can apply my expertise in a unique way.
- I have a passion for what I do and am energized by sharing it with others.
- Income from a speaking career is only limited by how hard I'm willing to work and by my creativity.
- A successful speaking career can lead to successful spinoff careers in writing and coaching.
- Speaking engagements can result in the chance to travel and in other opportunities for personal enrichment.

CHAPTER 16

Leading Travel Groups

If you love travel, history, culture, art, and working with people, a career as a tour guide could be a perfect fit. There are several options for working as a tour guide: You can work as a local guide (leading tours of local attractions to visiting tour groups); you can work as a traveling tour guide with a major tour company or cruise line; or you can design and lead your own tours. Not only are opportunities for travel-related careers plentiful, but the industry is also predicted to grow considerably as more and more Baby Boomers reach retirement.

Becoming a Local Guide

Of the three options, becoming a local guide is the easiest to break into. It could be as easy as designing your own informational tour about your hometown's attractions and marketing it to travel retailers (travel agents and tour companies) and the general public. Travel agencies and chambers of commerce may promote your services, or you can contract with major tour companies to be their permanent local "step-on" guide for your area. You'll have to do some research to find out which tour companies regularly tour your town, but it shouldn't be too difficult.

Becoming a Tour Director

If you want to get paid to travel abroad, you'll need to gain employment as a "tour director" or "tour escort" for a major company. Sign on with a company headquartered in your own country if you want to go abroad. This is easier than getting a work permit with a foreign company. It's likely that you'll be hired on as an independent contractor rather than as an employee, especially with smaller companies. Often, all of your expenses are paid (airfare, other travel costs, meals, hotels, etc.) and you'll also receive a per diem ($100–300 per day). In addition, tour escorts can expect to earn tips of around $5 per day, per guest (more if you're really good at establishing rapport with your clients).

Interestingly, most of the major tour companies do not have an employment or "careers" link on their websites. This is also true of cruise lines. Access to hiring information for tour companies and cruise lines can be had—at a price. There are several books, websites, and services specializing in job placement (or simply information brokering) for these types of companies. If you're serious about finding a job as a professional tour guide, however, paying as little as $5 (for a trial membership) shouldn't be a problem.

Become a Tour Reseller

Another option is to partner with a travel agency to find tours offering group discounts. If you want to travel to a specific destination and can find ten or more people to go with you, the travel agent can arrange for you (and a companion) to travel for free, as well as receive a small fee for each group member you sign up. This option is best suited for those who aren't interested in earning a living as a tour guide, but who love the idea of traveling for free.

Designing Your Own Tours

A final option is designing, marketing, and owning your own tour. This is the hardest of all options, but also the most potentially rewarding. Some states require tour operators to be licensed and bonded; check your local state's website for information. In either case, be prepared to have to deal with a lot of paperwork.

Skills and Training

The beauty of a second career as a tour director is that you'll likely be able to draw from much of the experience you already have: both professional and personal. In addition, you can choose to attend the industry's pre-eminent training institute, or bolster your skills through alternative methods.

The Institute

While there is no set standard for training and certification, getting trained by an organization such as the International Tour Management Institute can help land you a job with the major tour companies. The institute's program is fifteen days long and covers everything you need to know from becoming a city tour guide to leading tour groups on extended trips. The fifteenth day is dedicated to one-on-one counseling with regard to your individual career goals, as well as general job placement assistance (although the company makes no guarantee of future employment). The institute also hosts an annual symposium, where alumni can have brief "speed-dating length" interviews with the major tour providers. It's a chance for graduates to have that all-important face-to-face with potential employers.

More than 60 percent of the instruction is done outside the classroom aboard motor coaches, at the airport, and on board cruise ships in one- and two-day field trips. The cost of these field workshops is included in the tuition. Classes take place in San Francisco and occasionally in North Hollywood. The program costs $3,100, and portions of it may be tax deductible.

SUCCESS STORY

When Joanne Connors was a little girl, she truly believed she would someday see the entire world and meet all of the people in it. "I got off to a good start by becoming a flight attendant, and saw a lot of airports and a lot of hotels, but very little of the world."

Joanne's career as a flight attendant was short-lived, lasting only six months. During a strike to protest new requirements for flight engineers, Joanne became engaged to her childhood sweetheart, Ed. (At the time, flight attendants could not be engaged or married.)

After they married, Joanne dedicated the next two decades to raising her children. She felt that this should be her priority, and she'd make time to pursue her dreams after they'd entered adulthood.

Just before her youngest child turned twenty, Joanne had a major wake-up call. "A couple of my friends and former classmates died, and they were my age." She was in her late forties at this point. She remembers thinking, "Okay, I may not see the world, but at least I'd like to see the U.S. Please, God, at least the Grand Canyon!" She persuaded her husband to go on a bus tour of the Grand Canyon. "He thought I was crazy at first, but he went along." Joanne loved the experience, as did Ed, although for different reasons. "He was happy not to have to be the one driving or working out logistics!" Joanne, on the other hand, was fascinated by something else. "The Grand Canyon is one of the most awesome sights in the world, but there at the front of the bus was a sight almost as remarkable: a tour director, a woman being paid to travel." The experience lighted a fire in Joanne's heart that would soon lead to realization of her childhood dreams.

Not too long after they returned home to New England, a small ad in the *Boston Globe* caught her eye. It was for a one-day seminar for the International Tour Management Institute (ITMI). With the support of her children and Ed, Joanne made the call and signed up for the seminar.

After completing the one-day seminar, Joanne was accepted into the four-week training program, also held right there in Boston. Thanks to the networking made available by ITMI, she landed her first assignment right after graduating from the institute. On her first tour, she confesses, "I did everything wrong that you could!" Nevertheless, one tour led to another, and to another, and so on, until eventually Joanne's touring career took her to six of the seven continents, minus Antarctica. "I have climbed the foothills of the Himalayas in Nepal, walked the Great Wall of China, stood breathless in front of Machu Picchu in the Peruvian Andes, floated down the Nile on a barge, and been to Europe more times than I can count."

Having a sense of adventure is key to being a tour director, but so is a sense of humor. "I've been on tours where everything went wrong. On one tour, the river was too low for navigating, and it was a riverboat tour! On another, the boat started to sink and we had to abandon ship!"

But the biggest challenges of her profession arise from dealing with client personalities. "Many people get in this business thinking it's about travel. It's not. It's about people. You have to love people and know how to handle them. Traveling alone is one thing; traveling with thirty or forty people, all of whom have demands on your time, is another." Joanne says that it's absolutely vital for tour directors to find time in each tour to unwind and take care of themselves, away from the group. "It's a crucial part of survival," she says.

There's also another side to dealing with people as a tour director. "When you're in charge of leading a group, people see you in a different light. Whereas they normally wouldn't think twice about you in everyday life, when you're a tour director, suddenly you're the prettiest, brightest, funniest, and most patient person they know." If you're not careful, she says, "You can start to believe it!" Joanne's husband would usually give her twenty-four hours to come down off of the high from a tour. "Then he'd tap me on the shoulder and say, 'Excuse me, but I'm not on your tour. Now go make dinner.' Then I'd snap back to reality," she laughs. Touring is a wonderful world, she says, but "it's not the real world. You have to stay in the real world."

Another challenge of leading a successful career as a tour director is that if you're good at what you do, you can be gone a lot. It took Joanne three years to take charge of her schedule to the point where she could be selective about turning down tours. "I eventually started looking at my entire year in advance, being sure to put my family first." This is also crucial. While many successful tour directors are married, she says, "If there's anyone in your life you want to keep, you'd better be sure to keep a balanced schedule." Most of Joanne's tours were two weeks in duration, but occasionally, she'd take on longer trips, such as to Australia. "Those tours were often twenty-eight days, so then I'd be sure to be home for the next month."

This relates to another challenge: the effort of constantly reintegrating into one's own life. "The world doesn't stop just because you're off on a tour," she says. That is why maintaining a balanced schedule and having the support of your spouse and family are so important.

Today, Joanne has moved from touring to teaching the next generation of tour directors. "Teaching is an extension of my dream. It takes up all of those other wanderlust feelings that I had." ●

Other Programs and Skills to Consider

Community colleges also offer related courses, some of them even completely online. For example, the online course "Get Paid to Travel" lasts six weeks and costs only $139.

In addition to formal training, there are several other skills that will put you at an advantage: being able to speak a foreign language, planning and time management skills, public speaking, and being able to quickly and effectively take control of a crowd. Some of these skills you may already have; others can be supplemented through adult education courses at your local college or through private vendors.

The Importance of Doing Your Research

Whether you are leading local tours or leading a tour group on a multi-city tour, it's vital to research the area(s) you'll be touring extensively. Although the tour companies will provide basic information, it's a good idea to do your own homework.

Try to find quirky, offbeat, or humorous tidbits to add to your presentation; it will make a big difference in the group's enjoyment of the tour, as well as in their perception of you. This could lead to bigger tips and word-of-mouth recommendations from your clients. Examples of extra research include information on famous ghosts in the area, star-crossed lovers, famous duels or battles, or little-known historical facts. Perhaps the tidbit isn't about the place itself, but about a famous person who visited the site, and what they thought or said about it.

Developing a Specialty: The Importance of Value Added

Most people enjoy learning new and interesting things, and this is especially true of those who travel. In addition to taking the time to research different tidbits for each city you visit, you should also consider introducing your own particular area of expertise into your tours. Whether your previous career was in law, medicine, engineering, computers, science, teaching, or food, find a way to introduce this expertise into your tours. This will not only set you apart from the competition, but you'll be giving your groups added insight into an area that they were not expecting. They'll come away from the tour feeling like they got more than their money's worth. For example, one local guide in Marseilles who takes groups on a tour of a local winery also happens to have a degree in archaeology. His talks include not only information on the wines of the region (which the group expects) but also on the geology and archaeological finds in the area (which they do not). Most tour members leave that tour feeling that they got an exceptional value for their time and money.

PITFALLS AND PERILS Having a love of travel, culture, and the arts is definitely an asset, but it's not enough to be a good tour guide. Says one travel expert, "Make sure you have strong people skills as well as infinite patience." In addition, realize that you'll be around people for far longer than with most traditional jobs: up to eighteen hours each day. You'll be eating, drinking, traveling, and resting with a group of people, and they can never see you looking anything but happy and professional.

That said, realize that you will likely have very little, if any, time for yourself. You're primarily being paid to be present for others, so don't be disappointed when you can't fit in your own agenda.

It's also likely that on each trip, you'll have to deal with a crisis: anything from lost luggage, stolen passports, issues with customs officers, buses that break down, passengers having heart attacks or experiencing Montezuma's revenge, and much, much more. It's vital that you can a) keep calm in a crisis, no matter how grave, b) provide a reassuring presence, and c) think quickly on your feet. Joemy Wilson, a successful long-time tour director for Tauck World Discovery shares, "I love it when things go wrong. I love being the hero." She recalls one time when there was an issue with the local police on one of her tours. While her clients were visibly worried, she'd navigated similar circumstances before. "These things always work themselves out." At the end of the tour, her clients toasted her for her "unflappable" nature. When she asked what they were talking about, they reminded her of the incident (which had happened early in the tour). Her reply? "Oh, that." ●

Now, let's examine the concepts we've looked at in this chapter to see if right now, you feel that career as a tour guide is "worth it" to you. You may find it helpful to write down your thoughts in a notebook or to discuss these issues with your friends or family. As you answer each question, try to think of specific instances to support your opinion.

Checklist | Is It Worth It?

How many of these statements do you agree with?

○ I understand that being an effective tour guide is about more than being paid to travel.

○ Having adequate training is important, and I am willing to refine my skills to be competitive.

○ I love working with people: even when they are tired, angry, scared, and lost.

○ I understand that it's rare for things to go perfectly according to plan, but I am comfortable handling unexpected challenges.

○ I have a healthy sense of humor, can laugh at myself, and can maintain a positive attitude in the face of adversity.

If there are any statements you don't agree with, now is the time to carefully analyze the reasons why and determine how much of a roadblock this item represents in your overall plan.

SUMMARY YOU'D BE PERFECT FOR A CAREER AS A TOUR GUIDE BECAUSE:

- You have a love of travel, culture, and the arts.
- You enjoy speaking in front of crowds.
- You have special knowledge or a unique expertise to share with your groups.
- You're able to remain calm in a crisis and are an effective leader under any circumstances.
- You can think of nothing better than being paid to travel!

CHAPTER 17

Live to Eat: Culinary Careers

Are you known as a good cook among your friends and family? Do you spend your free time browsing new cookbooks or experimenting with new taste combinations in your kitchen? Have your family and friends come to expect a feast whenever you're in charge of a meal? If this sounds like you, you may be the right kind of person to launch a second career in the culinary arts.

There are many options available for foodies these days. You can become a food reviewer or blogger; open a specialty cooking supply store (online or brick-and-mortar); become a commercial cook; launch a catering business; become a personal chef; or open your own bakery, restaurant, or café.

The Litmus Test

One of the easiest ways to discover if a career in culinary arts is right for you is to test the waters in the kitchen of a franchise restaurant. You won't need any certifications and there are specific standards and recipes in place. Often, all you have to do is show up. Working as a line cook in a commercial restaurant will quickly give you a realistic assessment of whether or not this type of work is right for you.

How Eighty-Five Meatballs Changed My Life

As someone of Italian descent, I've had a life-long love of cooking. Food seems to define my life. I even have the habit of assessing the potential for new friendships by determining whether someone "eats to live, or lives to eat!" A few years into my corporate career, I took a sabbatical to explore some different career options. At one point, I was living in a communal home with fifteen other people as part of a volunteer trip on a wildlife expedition in Africa. Since the members of the expedition all had to take turns cooking, I was really looking forward to my turn. On the appointed day, I decided to make my mother's meatballs. After spending the entire morning in the kitchen to make eighty-five meatballs (which were quickly devoured), I realized that it was time to also make dinner. That's when it dawned on me that there's no way I could do this day after day. Thanks to this experience, I learned that for me, cooking will remain a beloved avocation shared with friends and family rather than a way to earn a living. Most importantly, I learned this before investing the time and expense to go to culinary school.

Culinary Schools

Even if you don't choose to become a professional chef, having some exposure to formal culinary arts training would be to your advantage in any food-related career. These days, it's not too difficult to find a culinary school nearby, and many also offer online courses for subjects such as food management and hospitality. It's impossible to attain a complete culinary degree online, but there are opportunities for those who already have some practical lab experience (i.e., an associate's degree or certificate from your community college) to complete a bachelor of culinary arts online. That said, bachelor's degrees are not required for success. Having an associate's degree, coupled with the right externship experience, is truly all you need, even to become a professional chef.

When choosing a school, you should first clearly define your goal. Do you want to become a professional chef at a high-end restaurant? In that case, a well-known school—such as Le Cordon Bleu Institute—is worth the investment. (Incidentally, you don't have to study at the institute itself. The Scottsdale Culinary Academy is one of many independent schools offering Cordon Bleu programs and certifications.) Or do you simply wish to have the skills to open your own café? In that case, your community college may even have a suitable program. Perhaps all you need is a class or two on food presentation in order to open your own catering business. Once again, attending a community college or taking a freestanding course at a culinary school may be all you need.

Licenses and Requirements

Like any business that has the potential to impact the health and well-being of others, cafés and restaurants must obtain licenses and pass several types of inspections. In addition, you'll be required to obtain several types of insurance.

The best starting place for information is your state restaurant industry association. In addition to adequate space requirements, you'll need to be aware of sanitation issues, smoking laws, noise restrictions, music licensing, payroll requirements, worker's compensation, liability and supplemental insurance, etc. Your business will also need to meet federal OSHA (Occupational Safety and Health Administration) requirements.

Commonly, your local health department will require your business to pass an opening inspection by a food safety specialist, along with a plumbing inspection. You'll receive a permit to operate, which will be reviewed yearly.

If you will be serving alcohol, you'll need to apply for a wine or liquor license. Requirements vary greatly by state and county. Some states still have "dry counties," where alcohol is prohibited, either all the time or during specific periods. You will need to ensure that your business is in compliance with all laws.

The best way to ensure your business is compliant with all applicable regulations is to create a detailed business plan and have it evaluated by someone knowledgeable in the trade. Your state restaurant board may be able to provide you with a consultant.

Employing Others

Depending on the size, scope, and success of your venture, you may eventually have to hire staff. Choose your staff with care; the person your clients meet when coming in the door matters as much as the quality of the food. Nothing can ruin an excellent meal like bad service.

Hiring others will involve payroll issues, the proper reporting of tips, effectively training your new hires, avoiding discrimination, complying with federal immigration laws, and dealing with disabilities.

The National Restaurant Association has some excellent resources available for dealing with human resource issues, including an excellent article on dealing with Generation X employees (who are likely to be your primary employment pool). This age group currently makes up 54 percent of the pool of restaurant workers, and they can either be the best employees you've ever had or the worst type of slackers. According to an article in *Restaurants USA*, it's all in how you manage them.

The Benefits of Simplicity

With all of the licenses, requirements, and restrictions opening a new café entails, your best approach is to start simply. What are the very best things you can offer? It's better to start with a few sure bets and build your business from there than it is to try to do too many things at once.

Customers like consistency. If you start out offering a particular meal or sandwich and it's a bestseller, you should think twice about taking it off the menu on whim, or to fit in a new idea. That's what specials are for.

One of the ways you can simplify your business (and your life) is to start out by offering limited hours. It may be too much to be open for breakfast, lunch, and dinner. When starting out, try just one. Then expand as interest, and the local competition, dictate.

Simplicity also works best in terms of décor, so do the most you can through the creative application of paint before investing money in fancy decorations. In the beginning, any extra income will need to be spent on advertising.

PITFALLS AND PERILS An article about starting a new restaurant business on eHow says it best: "Restaurants are simmering stockpots of potential accidents—from fires to floods to food poisoning and a hundred other potential horrors."

In addition, restaurants have a notoriously high failure rate. One small-town café that did everything right—from creating a delicious, reasonably priced menu to hiring the best possible staff—went out of business when a Cracker Barrel opened across the street. The location of your business is key: The best place is in an established neighborhood where the possible competitors are already known. While property in a growing area may be much cheaper to lease than property in an established area, you also face a greater threat from the unknown. What's to stop a national chain from moving in next door? Another risk is that a business could move in that completely conflicts with the image you're trying to convey. For example, you could open a European wine bar, only to have a multicolored, Dr. Seuss–themed children's dentist move into the same complex.

Another potential pitfall that seems to affect successful businesses is complacency. Examples abound of restaurant owners who've jumped through all of the legal hoops, made the right investments in advertising and publicity, and built a loyal clientele who then seem to throw it all away through a complacent attitude.

Part of battling complacency is ensuring that you stay ahead of the trends in your industry. You may have been doing something a certain way your entire life, but it's important to keep up on what's going on in the rest of the world. Not to say that you have to follow every fad, but you do need to develop a knack for determining what is a transient fad and what is here to stay. A perfect example is the emergence of the Atkins diet and subsequent desire for "low-carb" foods. While the Atkins diet may have come and gone, there is still a significant portion of the population that looks for foods low in carbohydrates as a permanent aspect of their diet. The same is true of offering vegetarian or vegan options.

On top of everything else, it's important to recognize that client-driven industries such as cafés can only be successful if they provide a convenience for the client. That said, expect to work long hours and sacrifice evenings, weekends, and holidays if you truly expect to be successful. ●

SUCCESS STORY

Carla Lucente grew up in Fort Washington, Maryland. Her love of food began at a young age while working in her parents' Italian restaurant. After several years working in finance and construction, Carla decided to follow her dream and attend culinary school at Baltimore International College. Following graduation, Carla started her own catering business and began working part-time at Trader Joe's grocery store in Annapolis.

While working at Trader Joe's, Carla met Stacey Jackowski, another native of Maryland. Stacey shared Carla's life-long love of food, having grown up surrounded by food on her grandparents' farm and her vegan parent's extensive backyard garden. The culmination of these experiences eventually led her to Johnson and Wales University's culinary program in Rhode Island. While still attending college, Stacey worked at Trader Joe's and began helping Carla with her catering business.

After a few years of cooking together, they decided to open a restaurant of their own. They called it b.b. Bistro—the best of the best Annapolis had to offer. Carla began searching for the perfect place. Stacey began designing the logo. They printed a few commercial real estate listings in the Annapolis area. They looked at several potential locations, but when they pulled up to the big yellow house in West Annapolis, they knew they had found the perfect spot. Stacey exclaimed, "I've always dreamed of having a restaurant in a yellow house!" They both jumped out of the car and ran to the huge glass front to peer in. "It's perfect!" said Carla. Within three months, they signed a lease, and b.b. Bistro was born.

Stacey and Carla's strengths complemented each other perfectly. Stacey's background in art coupled with Carla's experience in construction enabled the pair to act as the general contractors as well as the designers of their own restaurant. With help from "handy" friends and family, they constructed the kitchen and coffee bar area. They repaired drywall and painted.

In a smart business strategy, Carla and Stacey use as many local vendors as possible. Each Saturday, they visit the local farmer's market to purchase the week's supplies. They support their neighbors by purchasing locally grown produce and herbs. (They also grow their own herbs, peppers, and tomatoes in a garden in the front of the bistro.) All of their kitchen scraps are fed to the chickens at the farm that produces their eggs. The business is also part of the "green" movement; they compost their coffee grounds and recycle all of their bottles and cardboard. Thanks to these efforts, their business only produces one large can of garbage per week.

Stacey and Carla make all of their soups, salads, sandwiches, quiche, and salad dressings from scratch each day. The bistro's menu is a blend of home-style, diner, Mediterranean, and vegetarian cuisine. Stacey's Granola Bars and Carla's Flourless Chocolate Ganache Cake are customer favorites. They bake fresh muffins and make their own croutons. Everything is fresh—the restaurant does not have a freezer.

Despite being launched during an economic downturn, the b. b. Bistro has flourished. Stacey and Carla's success is due to their strong partnership and the warm welcome they have received from the West Annapolis community. They have an abundance of loyal, regular customers. Several come twice a day, once in the morning for coffee and an egg and cheese sandwich, and again in the afternoon for organic iced tea, homemade soup, and delicious panini. Carla and Stacey know most of their customers by name and are quick to recognize and welcome a new one.

Another way Stacey and Carla have managed to connect with the community is by hosting several types of local events. These include story time with face painting on Friday mornings, an open mike poetry night, a regular Celtic music night, a monthly art show and reception for local artists, and author book talks and signings. To aid their growing business, the partners also offer catering, free local delivery, and special-occasion space rentals.

For Carla and Stacey, operating their own bistro is the culmination of years of dreaming, planning, training, and hard work. But when they walk up to their little yellow house every day to go to work, they know it's been worth it. ●

Now, let's examine the concepts we've looked at in this chapter to see if right now, you feel a career in the culinary arts is "worth it" to you. You may find it helpful to write down your thoughts in a notebook or to discuss these issues with your friends or family. As you answer each question, try to think of specific instances to support your opinion.

Checklist | Is It Worth It?

How many of these statements do you agree with?

○ Opening a café involves compliance with multiple regulations, from the federal to local level.

○ Choosing and retaining staff can be challenging, and there are multiple federal laws that must be followed, from disability to immigration.

○ I understand that restaurants have a very high failure rate.

○ I'm willing to spend long hours on my feet in a mostly uncomfortable (hot and cramped) environment.

○ I have the attention to detail necessary to practice extreme caution with regard to food safety.

○ I'm willing to attend culinary school to refine my skills.

If there are any statements you don't agree with, now is the time to carefully analyze the reasons why and determine how much of a roadblock this item represents in your overall plan.

SUMMARY YOU'RE READY TO OPEN YOUR OWN CAFÉ BECAUSE:

- You have a love of food that is unmatched by your peers.
- You have researched the local, state, and federal requirements.
- Your business plan has been vetted by an expert in the field.
- You've made use of the many resources offered by your state restaurant association and by its national counterpart.
- You have attended culinary school or are currently in the process of likewise refining your skills.
- You've successfully completed an externship or worked as a line cook for a commercial franchise.
- You have a plan in place to stay ahead of the trends.
- You understand the risks but are ready to make your mark on the culinary world!

CHAPTER 18

Real Estate, Insurance, and Finance

If you possess a penchant for sales, strong attention to detail, a creative approach to advertising your services, and an analytical mind, you could have a very successful career in real estate, insurance, or financial planning or advising. While there are certainly plenty of Realtors who are not analytical, and financial planners who are not strong salespeople, the most successful professionals in these fields possess some combination of all four attributes.

Do You Have What It Takes?

Real estate, insurance, and financial careers have several things in common. First, they offer the opportunity for those with an entrepreneurial spirit to work in a structured, yet independent business. In each case, you're likely to be working as an agent for a larger brokerage, although opportunities do exist for financial planners to work purely on their own. Each of these professions also involves working with individuals on matters of great personal importance.

Since these types of careers all require a significant up-front investment and the establishment of a solid customer base before becoming profitable, they are best suited to those who have retirement funds from previous careers in public service, the military, teaching, or the like. There is actually a big upside to embarking on any of these careers as an older individual: You have a more trustworthy appearance. Whereas in other careers you might find yourself faced with some element of age discrimination, in this instance the opposite is true. Older people who sell products are not only perceived as more trustworthy, but as more knowledgeable as well!

Licenses and Requirements

To obtain a license in insurance or real estate, most states require applicants to complete prelicensing courses; an examination regarding general fundamentals; and a state-specific exam for the state in which you wish to practice.

Licensee requirements vary considerably by state, and many states do not have reciprocity agreements. That means that if you plan on operating in more than one state, you'll likely have to be separately licensed in all of them.

Financial planners, on the other hand, are not required to have a license or any other specific certification. That said, you probably won't get too far in a career handling other people's money if you don't have some form of credentials. There are three approaches to earning these credentials. You could apply for a job with a large employer such as

Thrivent Financial, Edward Jones, or American Express, which will put you through training (often while paying you a basic salary). You would then go on to take one of the exams offered by the Financial Industry Regulatory Authority.

Alternatively, you could pursue a degree from one of approximately 285 colleges and universities that offer preparation for the Certified Financial Planner Exam. After obtaining the CFP designation—which requires three years of qualifying full-time work experience—you'll promise to follow a set of ethics and meet continuing-education requirements.

While Realtors and insurance agents earn their living based on commissions, financial planners may either work for a fee or for a commission. Those who earn commissions on the products they sell are known as financial advisors instead of financial planners.

For real estate agents, acquiring your license is only the first step. If you plan on showing resale homes to clients, you'll also need to join your local board in order to have access to the Multiple Listing Service. Membership fees for these organizations can be significant.

Real Estate Specialists

Realtors can choose to specialize in either residential or commercial real estate, or even in time-share sales. Residential agents specialize in working with homeowners, while commercial agents deal with office space and buildings. In most states, the general real estate salesperson license allows you to do both, but in real estate, the top performers are those who specialize. If you can bill yourself as the expert in a narrow field, you're likely to be at an advantage.

Residential Versus Commercial

Residential real estate tends to require more of a 24-7 mentality; you never know when your phone is going to ring and someone wants to see a property! Evenings and weekends are prime working times, as are holidays. If you're a listing agent, expect to spend many a weekend showing an "Open House." If you're a buyer's agent, expect to be run ragged looking at dozens of listings with clients—who often ask to go back to "see that one again." Commercial Realtors, on the other hand, tend to have more of a nine-to-five schedule, although not 100 percent of the time. Commercial real estate can also involve more complex legal issues, and the transaction times can be significantly greater, often by several months.

Time-Share Sales

Another path you can take in real estate is selling time-share properties, or "vacation ownership." Though the industry has a rather disreputable past, things have changed considerably in recent years. Virtually all of the major hotel chains have branched out into time-sharing, mostly as a way to increase brand recognition and loyalty. Hyatt Corporation, for instance, makes the vast majority of its revenue from its hotel operations, but got into the time-share industry after all of its competitors did. As one salesperson explains it, "If you own a Hyatt vacation property, you're more likely to think of Hyatt the next time you book a hotel." Not only that, but so are your kids and grandkids. As Henry Ford discovered, brand loyalty is something that can be passed on through the generations.

Time-share sales can be an extremely profitable career. However, you have to be very skilled at sales and able to overcome people's objections, whether they voice them or not. "Most people come into the presentation purely for the gift," a time-share trainer shares. "But once they're sitting in front of you, you have to quickly penetrate their defenses and get to their real objections." The nice thing about time-share sales versus traditional real estate is that the leads come to you. There is no prospecting. Also, you just have to get to know one product and report to work in one place. "There's none of that driving around trying to find properties or sitting for hours at an open house for a client," says one salesperson. While all of this is true, some people don't like the high pressure inherent in most time-share settings.

SUCCESS STORY

At the age of fifty-eight and a half, Paul decided to cash in his chips from the airline industry and retire one and a half years early. "I could tell what was coming down the pipeline, and it didn't look good." After thirty-one years as a commercial pilot, he retired early and moved with his wife to Sedona, Arizona.

An avid hiker, Paul initially spent his days hiking the red rocks and discovering the area. His wife, Lynne, a successful travel writer, soon got busy with her writing. Between needing to "get out from under her feet" and wanting to supplement his pension, the couple decided it was time for him to look for a job. "Real estate popped into mind as a great second career choice," so Paul signed up for the prelicensing course.

At first, he was pretty sure he'd like to go into residential real estate. But after meeting with a few of the area firms, he wasn't really thrilled with what he heard. With his degree in mechanical engineering, he'd also briefly considered continuing on with his studies to become an appraiser. When he found out that option would have involved a two-year apprenticeship in Phoenix (ninety miles away), he said "No, thank you."

Meanwhile, he was approached by a couple of the local time-share companies (of which Sedona has several). After hearing what they had to offer (mostly high-pressure environments), he decided it wasn't for him. When he heard about a career day at the Hyatt, he went in for an interview.

As a time-share owner himself, Paul was immediately impressed with the Hyatt product. "I can sell that. It would be easy," he told himself. He was right. His people skills were excellent, his approach low-key, and his background as a pilot impressive to most people. Those three factors, combined with his genuine enthusiasm for the product, launched Paul's new career into the stratosphere. He has managed to average over $1 million in sales both years he's been selling, even in a downward-spiraling economy.

Recently, he was promoted to in-house sales, meaning that he works exclusively with owners. Paul is enjoying his new role immensely, even though the hours are longer. "I love it when you meet new owners and they are so happy with the product," Paul says. One client told Paul, "I bought this product so it would force me to vacation, and it worked. I vacationed more last year than I did in the previous ten years combined. Now I'm back to buy one of these for my kids so I can pass on this legacy of better living to them." This year, Paul is once again set to gross over $1 million in sales, despite taking two months off to travel with his wife.

Paul's advice to those considering a career in time-share? "If you're going to do it, really do it. Know your product backwards and forwards." The next key is really hearing what people are saying. "You need to be able to discern exactly what people want, what is best for them. Don't just sell them a one-size-fits-all product," Paul says, "sell them a solution." ●

Insurance — Generalists

Insurance agents, on the other hand, are usually not specialists. Typically, an agent sells one or more types of insurance: property and casualty, life, health, disability and long-term care insurance. Insurance can be sold to individuals as well as to businesses, and there is also a separate niche within the field of insurance to process manufacturer warranties and claims. The major benefit of a career in insurance is that the need for its products remains strong despite dips and turns in the overall economy.

Financial Planners — Specialists

Financial planners can offer generalized services, but usually specialize in either retirement planning or debt reduction. Some financial planners do both, but only advertise one or the other service to specific markets. Since you'll be dealing with people's lifelong investments and savings, it's crucial to stay on top of the latest laws and regulations. For this reason alone, specialization often makes sense.

PITFALLS AND PERILS All three of these careers tend to be strongly impacted by the business cycle, although those who are truly successful have the ability to shift their area of concentration as needed. For example, Realtors might specialize in new home sales when the market is strong, then shift to foreclosure sales in an economic downturn. Insurance agents might specialize in health products in times of plenty, but shift focus to life insurance and asset protection when times are uncertain. Financial planners can focus on investment advice when markets are strong, but turn to debt consolidation or reduction when markets are shaky.

Not only are these career choices sensitive to economic fluctuations, but like any sales-driven career, they are also subject to their own cycles. Even the most successful agents and planners can have one spectacular month followed by two dismal months. Those with commission-based careers need to learn to plan for these fluctuations very carefully. Your income may not come in with regularity, but you can bet that your bills still will.

Another aspect these career choices have in common, but that you may not realize, is that people have to like you before they will buy from you. In fact, people are inclined to buy *anything* from someone they truly like. That said, don't try too hard: phonies are easy to spot, and you don't want to come across as "slick." The key to success here is to be yourself and to find something to like about the other person. If you can do this quickly, it's easy to then establish rapport and close the sale. On the other hand, you don't want to spend too much time befriending someone instead of selling them.

If you are seriously considering earning your livelihood through a sales-oriented career, there are several excellent sales training programs available. It's worth the investment (often several hundred dollars) to acquire such a program and follow it carefully. ●

Non-Sales Alternatives

If you're not into sales, you can also pursue other types of careers in these fields. Those interested in either real estate or insurance could pursue a career as an appraiser.

In real estate, some couples enjoy working together as property managers for apartment complexes or storage units. Other insurance-related fields include adjusters and claim processors. In the world of finance, you could pursue debt counseling for a social services agency.

Now, let's examine the concepts we've looked at in this chapter to see if right now, you feel a career in insurance, financial planning, or real estate is "worth it" to you. You may find it helpful to write down your thoughts in a notebook or to discuss these issues with your friends or family. As you answer each question, try to think of specific instances to support your opinion.

Checklist | Is It Worth It?

How many of these statements do you agree with?

○ Sales are my strong suit: people trust and like me.

○ I can weather the cyclical nature of a sales-based career.

○ I understand the importance and benefit of advanced training in sales.

○ I am prepared to deal with the moral dilemmas and sensitive information common to these types of careers.

○ I am willing to invest time and money to obtain and stay current with related licenses, dues, and professional association fees.

If there are any statements you don't agree with, now is the time to carefully analyze the reasons why and determine how much of a roadblock this item represents in your overall plan.

SUMMARY YOU'RE READY FOR A CAREER IN REAL ESTATE, INSURANCE, OR FINANCIAL PLANNING BECAUSE:

- You're an entrepreneur at heart.
- You enjoy working with people on the big issues in their lives.
- You have a strong sense of personal integrity and service.
- You're willing to weather the cyclical nature of these types of careers.
- You have a solid educational background and a professional demeanor.
- You would most enjoy a career that has structure, while allowing for personal freedom in terms of hours and expectations.

CHAPTER 19

Serving Others: Social Work

Social work is a broad category that encompasses many subspecialties: working with children, prisoners, the disabled, the mentally challenged, substance abusers, those facing unemployment or other life-altering circumstances, or with those facing debilitating or terminal diseases. Typically, a person will enter a career in social work already passionate about a specific cause.

A World of Opportunity

Opportunities for social workers exist at local hospitals, schools, nursing homes, state run institutions, and nonprofit groups specializing in providing support to victims of crimes. The majority of positions fall under the governmental umbrella. In addition, there are opportunities to work internationally for organizations such as the United Nations and the International Red Cross.

While the minimum degree necessary for a career in social work is a bachelor's in social work, a master's in social work (or related field) has now become the standard. Entry into a master's program does not require a bachelor's degree in social work, but courses in psychology, biology, sociology, economics, political science, and social work are recommended. A second language can also be very helpful, especially Spanish.

According to the Bureau of Labor Statistics, career opportunities in social work are projected to grow much faster than average, a total increase of 22 percent through the year 2010. There will be a particular need for workers in rural areas. As the number of Baby Boomers reaching retirement rises, so does the need for more social workers. As a result, the National Association of Social Workers (NASW) reports a major shortage in workers.

The Right Motivation

If your primary objective is to help others improve their lives, a career as a social worker could be right for you. This career attracts people of many different backgrounds, from corporate executives to police officers. In fact, over 60 percent of current social workers are second-career social workers, according to a study by the National Association of Social Workers (NASW). Of these, just over half came from jobs in the private sector, and roughly a quarter each from the public and nonprofit sectors.

The *Boston Globe* recently featured a story on people leaving corporate careers behind to find fulfillment through social work. The School of

Social Work at Simmons College is just one of the schools witnessing a surge in the number of older students pursing career changes into social work. Most of these students find that they are able to apply their previous professional skills and backgrounds to social work as well, bringing more to the table as a result.

SUCCESS STORY

Maura never imagined that, at age fifty-eight, she would find a way to improve a major public health crisis that claims the life and health of so many Americans. Annually, more than 250,000 persons die because they simply get "mixed up" with their medications and inadvertently use them incorrectly, or do not take them at all. As a pharmacist, this troubled her greatly—but only when she abandoned that profession did she find a way to help the ill and elderly avoid these common mistakes in their daily lives.

Maura's first career was as a Roman Catholic nun, "with all its altruistic dreams of helping others." The convent trained her to be a pharmacist, a profession serving her thirty years after she returned to lay life. "But the aspect of pharmacy I loved—working with patients and families—slowly devolved into almost all administrative and technical tasks," Maura shares. Work became tedious and routine.

Maura's life-changing moment came with a diagnosis of breast cancer. "The deep depression following treatment provided one good thing: time to think. Had the pebble of my life fallen into the waters of existence and made a ripple? Not yet." Maura decided that she needed meaningful work.

"Social work popped to mind—I could help individuals and families change to create the lives they desire. The profession is age-friendly, allowing social workers to work well into their later years. So what if I depleted my not-too-hefty retirement savings?"

A friend protested her decision: "But you'll be fifty-eight when you graduate!" Maura reminded her that she would be fifty-eight anyway—so why not be enjoying a new profession?

Acceptance into a local master's degree program proved daunting, with 2,000 applicants competing for 200 places. "I improved my odds by acing two undergraduate social work classes at a junior college, entered the University of Kansas Master of Social Work program, and—four grueling years later—proudly added MSW, then LCSW behind my name: I was a licensed clinical social worker, a psychotherapist. It was the best decision of my life."

"Working in three distinct professions—as a social worker, a psychotherapist, and a pharmacist—offered insight into tackling one of the most difficult problems facing medicine today: Why can't people take medications regularly? Sixty years of medical research in this area has failed to offer solutions due to the incorrect assumption that educating patients creates lifestyle change." Instead, Maura discovered that people do not change by being educated by someone else or doing "what the doctor ordered," but by choosing what they want to do because it fits into their life scheme and supports their self-image.

By applying the techniques of all three professions, Maura not only launched a successful career in social work, but a program that will improve the lives of others for years to come. And she did it all after the age of fifty-eight! ●

The Right Personality: Can You Leave Work at Work?

Social workers are a vital link for patients between hospitalization/rehabilitation and their return to being normal and productive members of the community. Individuals interested in this field need to have the ability to establish relationships with a wide range of people. In addition, they should feel comfortable interviewing individual clients and families in order to assess the physical, social, and psychological needs of a patient. Doing this well requires the ability to evaluate a variety of information in order to reach a conclusion regarding the nature and degree of a client's problems.

Of paramount importance, social workers must also be able to relate to people without having a patient's problems overwhelm them.

PITFALLS AND PERILS While social work is tremendously rewarding, it can also be emotionally taxing. As a social worker, you will by the very nature of the job see things that most people aren't exposed to: victims of abuse, disease, crimes, and circumstance.

A common complaint from social workers is in regard to frustration with the laws against abuse, incest or rape, and the reality that not all cases can be won. "You'll see some pretty violent things that you would never expect to see," says Wendy, who works with abused children.

Another potential pitfall is the expectation of being able to resolve everything all at once. "Some situations take a lot of time to resolve. Be patient and know that it is worth it to hang in there," Wendy shares.

In a similar vein, the Women's Justice Center website has this to say about the importance of social workers: "One of the reasons your role is so vital is that the agencies and individuals your clients will be dealing with generally have fragmented responsibilities. Most likely no one individual will be overseeing the big picture. So even if the only thing you do is monitor your client's case and make sure she doesn't fall through the cracks, you can save her life literally and figuratively."

In addition to the challenges presented by the nature of the cases themselves, there are also several indirect stressors in the life of a social worker. The most commonly cited problems by social workers include mismanagement by those not on the front lines, fear of downsizing and budget cuts (common for those working for government agencies), office and interagency politics, lack of appreciation, work schedules that blur work and personal time, mountains of paperwork and red tape, and increased personal risk.

According to an article on the support website *www.FriedSocialWorker .com*, "Dangerous situations are common for psych social workers and child protective workers. Medical and prison social workers often face patients with airborne-communicable diseases such as TB without being informed of the risk and without adequate protective masks. Social workers frequently must interact with clients on a crisis basis without security staff or basic safety precautions. In our opinion, nothing else more clearly communicates an employer's lack of appreciation and respect than to jeopardize social workers in this way during the course of our work day." ●

Now, let's examine the concepts we've looked at in this chapter to see if right now, you feel a career in social work is "worth it" to you. You may find it helpful to write down your thoughts in a notebook or to discuss these issues with your friends or family. As you answer each question, try to think of specific instances to support your opinion.

Checklist | Is It Worth It?
How many of these statements do you agree with?

○ I understand that social work involves dealing with victims of abuse, disease, crimes, and circumstance.

○ I am willing to work long hours, be on call, or sacrifice evenings, weekends, and some holidays in order to make a difference in someone's life.

○ I understand that social work has a high rate of burnout due to the direct and indirect challenges of the job, but I am willing to give it my best shot for as long as I can.

If there are any statements you don't agree with, now is the time to carefully analyze the reasons why and determine how much of a roadblock this item represents in your overall plan.

If you have a strong desire to help others but either don't want to get a degree in social work or would prefer to use your current professional skills in a different application, you can apply for a closely related job or volunteer position such as a caseworker aide, prison visitor, Meals on Wheels driver, hospice volunteer, outreach worker, or a crisis center clerk.

SUMMARY SOCIAL WORK IS RIGHT FOR ME BECAUSE:

- I have a strong desire to make a difference in the lives of others.
- I am a compassionate person who is also able to practice detachment.
- Knowing that I made a difference in someone's life is worth more to me than praise or monetary gain.
- I understand that, many times, all people need to turn their life around is someone who cares.

CHAPTER 20

Serving Your Community: Law Enforcement

Opportunities to work in law enforcement are as distinct as they are plentiful: You could consider a career as a police officer, sheriff's deputy, parole officer, federal agent, state trooper, air marshal, or marine enforcement officer. Two things all of these careers require in common are a high level of physical fitness and high moral standing.

A career in law enforcement might be right for you if you have a strong desire to serve your community, enjoy variety in your work, and thrive on challenges. Law enforcement careers also typically offer great pay, good benefits (including retirement), and job security. In many communities, there is also an element of prestige associated with law enforcement, especially at the federal level.

Can You Make the Grade?

Entry requirements for these types of positions differ depending on which avenue of law enforcement you pursue, as well as by state or county. If you elect to become a police officer, you have to pass a written civil service test, followed by hearing, vision, strength, and physical agility tests. The next level of testing includes a background investigation, a lie detector examination, and a psychological evaluation. If you make it past these hurdles, you may be invited to attend a police academy.

If you're interested in working for a federal agency (such as the FBI, the Secret Service, the Drug Enforcement Agency, or the Border Patrol) expect to follow similar steps, but the background investigation will be far more intensive, involving interviews with anyone who knows you (even spouses you've divorced within the last ten years). In addition to verifying your employment history, expect your neighbors to be interviewed, your credit history pulled, and anything you've ever done to be revealed. This probably won't be the type of career change you can execute in total secrecy, at least not without raising a few eyebrows.

In addition, a bachelor's degree is required to become a federal agent. Some agencies may also have maximum age restrictions in place, but this may vary depending on your background and the agency's needs.

It's Not *Law and Order* or *CSI*

Thanks to realistic television dramas such as the ones named above, there is a lot of misinformation about law enforcement careers. Even when the technical details are portrayed accurately on these shows, viewers are more often than not left with a faulty perception of reality. Law enforcement careers certainly have their high-octane moments, but there is also a lot of tedium and precision work. New recruits are often astounded by the number of specific procedures that must be followed to the letter. Real-life mavericks don't make it far in this career choice, in direct contrast to life in the movies.

One of the biggest misconceptions portrayed by television dramas is the concept that justice is neat. The criminal commits a crime, the law enforcement officer follows the clues and makes an arrest, and order is eventually restored at a trial. For many law enforcement officers, reality often stands in stark contrast to that scenario. Instead, despite doing everything right, law enforcement officers frequently show up in the courtroom only to watch the person they apprehended get off on a technicality. This is potentially the biggest source of frustration and on-the-job stress faced by those in this profession.

With these types of factors in mind, it's vital that you take the advice in Chapter 8 and go on several "ride-alongs" if you are considering a career in law enforcement. You should also talk to as many people as you can in this line of work before committing your time and resources to a career that may not be a good match for your personality.

Acknowledging the Risks

While not every moment may be filled with adventure, law enforcement is a dangerous profession. According to the FBI, 59,000 police officers were assaulted in 2007. Nearly one-third of these assaults occurred in response to "disturbance calls," which includes everything from bar brawls to domestic violence. Fifty-seven officers were "feloniously killed" in that same year, fifty-five with firearms and two with vehicles being used as a weapon. In contrast, eighty-three officers died in accidents, forty-nine of which were motor vehicle accidents.

When it comes to federal agents, the fatality rates are lower, but being killed in action isn't the only risk those with careers in law enforcement have to worry about. Even in situations where no one is actively trying to harm you, there are increased indirect risks to your health and well-being. One example is exposure to diseases such as hepatitis or HIV in the process of apprehending a suspect or at the scene of an accident.

PITFALLS AND PERILS The dangerous elements of a career in law enforcement have the potential to affect not just the person holding the job, but that person's family as well. When undercover vice officer R. T. turned state's evidence against a local restaurateur for drug trafficking, he had no idea his work would literally follow him home. Shortly after the bust, the department received word from an informant that the defendant had hired two out-of-state hit men to kill R. T. and his family, and they were able to track the killers down and stop them before anything happened. On another occasion, a defense attorney openly used the threat of harm to R. T.'s family as an intimidation device by asking, "Officer, please state your address for the record." R. T. refused to give his home address, but instead said, "For the safety of my family I decline to answer that." The defense attorney replied, "That's okay, officer, we already know where you live."

On a less dramatic note, law enforcement and a regular schedule do not go hand in hand. You should expect long hours and nontraditional work schedules, which may prove inconvenient for your spouse or other family members. If your mate is also involved in shift work, this can really tax a relationship. Some federal agents enjoy more regular hours but can expect to be abruptly called out of town (or out of the country) for long periods at a time.

Aside from physical danger to your family, there is also the danger that your relationship may not withstand the stresses of police life. While there are no official data on divorce rates for law enforcement personnel, it's easy to see how a high-stress job coupled with long and irregular hours could lead to relationship strife.

Another potential pitfall of a law enforcement career is the social stigma that accompanies the profession. Many people have an attitude of fear when it comes to police officers, and you may find that friendships are difficult to form. In addition, police academies often warn recruits that you will likely lose your existing friends in the transition.

At the other end of the spectrum are those who would take advantage of your position of authority for their own gain. These requests could range from relatively benign requests to fix a speeding ticket to outright criminal misuse of authority.

It's no wonder, then, why it's easy for those in law enforcement to adopt a rather jaundiced view of the world and to find it difficult to trust anyone other than their immediate families. This profession carries with it a high risk of depression and alcoholism as a result.

Finally, as a living instrument of the law, you must maintain the highest level of propriety in all of your relationships. You should therefore expect to be closely watched by those in your community, your peers, and superiors. ●

SUCCESS STORY

When Jack decided to leave his teaching job at Ohio State University behind to be with his fiancée in her small western hometown, he didn't hesitate for a minute. After all, he had a PhD in Russian history and a successful career as a college professor. How hard could it be to find similar work?

Shortly after he arrived in town, he indeed found work quickly. The current history teacher at one of the local colleges was on sabbatical, so Jack was able to pick up her entire course load for a semester. At first, he thought things were progressing rather well. Then he received his first paycheck. Although he had a full course load, the school was paying him as an adjunct instructor, which was not enough to survive on, let alone support a family. Fortunately, his fiancée was working as a nurse and had a good income, so she was able to provide for them both. The couple got married and adopted a wait and see attitude. Jack decided to keep teaching as an adjunct until one of the full-time professors retired, with the hope that he'd be offered a full-time position.

Eventually, one of the professors did retire, but due to budgetary constraints the school replaced him with two adjuncts. After that, Jack decided to regroup and consider his options. A move was out of the question because his wife had joint custody of two high-school-aged children, and her ex-husband wasn't amenable to the family moving out of town. With those considerations, Jack had to find a way to earn a living in that town, at least for now. With a minimal investment, he started his own landscaping company and spent the next two years engaged in hard physical labor. While his business was successful in attracting clients, it was grueling work and paid about the same as teaching at the community college. His frustration level began to grow.

Then one day, Jack turned on the radio as he was driving home from a job. "There was a commercial from the town saying they needed police officers. I thought, why not?" He called the town and got the process going.

His wife was supportive. Though she had never complained about his inadequate pay, Jack was sure that she'd be much happier with their situation if he found a better-paying job.

Although he was in great shape thanks to his landscaping job, Jack remembers being nervous about his age (he was now forty-eight) throughout the entire application process. What if they told him he was too old?

Since no one brought it up, neither did Jack. He took the physical exam, the written exam, and the health tests. He submitted his information for the background check. Finally, he was admitted to the academy. It eventually dawned on him that that age might be a protected class. "I spent my entire working life classified as a White Anglo-Saxon Protestant Male. I never figured that affirmative action would one day work in my favor!" Jack laughs.

After spending seventeen weeks at the police academy, Jack began actual on-the-job training. This was the first time he questioned his choice. "On one of my very first shifts after the academy, I was put on the graveyard shift. This is when all of the bad stuff happens in a small town, and those working the shift were a bunch of very young, very gruff guys with a lot of bravado. I remember looking at these guys in the room and thinking, 'What have I gotten myself into?' I wasn't even sure these guys were the good guys," Jack shares. However, the feeling proved short-lived.

In fact, one of the main things Jack enjoys about his career change into police work as opposed to teaching is precisely "the feeling of camaraderie among the officers. Teaching is a fairly solitary job," he confesses.

When asked if it was difficult transitioning from an intellectual career in academia to police work, Jack has a surprising answer: "Not at all. Police work is so multifaceted, it's not just knowing the law. In my job, I deal with criminal behavior, psychology, firearms, detection, and much more. Intellectually it's been challenging as well as satisfying."

That said, police work is not for everyone. "My wife's a nurse. Both nurses and police officers see things that most people wouldn't want to see. You're dealing with bad people living tragic lives." While a person may be able to handle seeing the ugly side of society, Jack cautions, they may not really want to have to deal with it on a daily basis.

Today, Jack is still enjoying his career as a police officer and is working on getting into the detective side of things. "I still have a lot to learn as a patrol officer, but I'm excited about the possibility."

Although the stepchildren are now out of high school and the couple is free to move, Jack has found his niche. Despite the fact that this was a career choice he was practically forced into, Jack has no regrets. "I think having to try something radically different has been good for me. It forced me to get out of my rut. Starting over from scratch has been humbling but renewing." Changing careers in middle age reinvigorates you mentally and physically, Jack says. "You get your youth back." ●

Now, let's examine the concepts we've looked at in this chapter to see if right now, you feel a career in law enforcement is "worth it" to you. You may find it helpful to write down your thoughts in a notebook or to discuss these issues with your friends or family. As you answer each question, try to think of specific instances to support your opinion.

Checklist | Is It Worth It?

How many of these statements do you agree with?

○ I am personally prepared to work long hours and nontraditional work schedules.

○ I understand that a career in law enforcement involves considerable physical, emotional, and mental risks.

○ My mate is willing to accept the dangerous aspects of my job.

○ I can cope with the fact that there will be occasions when—through no fault of my own—justice will not be carried out.

○ I understand that a career in law enforcement may change the way I am perceived by others, as well as the way I perceive the world.

○ I understand that law enforcement is primarily about procedure and not about drama.

○ I feel confident I'll be able to resist the temptations that might arise from being in a position of authority.

If there are any statements you don't agree with, now is the time to carefully analyze the reasons why and determine how much of a roadblock this item represents in your overall plan.

SUMMARY A CAREER IN LAW ENFORCEMENT IS RIGHT FOR ME BECAUSE:

- I have a strong desire to serve my community.
- I am physically fit.
- I place a high value on moral authority.
- I am able to maintain my cool in extreme situations.
- Precision and order are important to me.
- I am not bothered by uncertainty, but rather am intrigued by a career in which no day is truly the same.
- I am willing to trade personal safety for job security and good benefits.

CHAPTER 21

Serving Your Country: The Military

In the wake of the September 11, 2001, attacks, the military witnessed a resurgence in interest from a wide variety of people wanting to serve their country. Individuals of all backgrounds, professions, and ages visited their local recruiters, stirred by feelings of patriotism. Although national interest has somewhat abated since that time, there are many reasons a second career in the military could be right for you.

Benefits of Joining as an Officer

If you like the idea of challenging work, discipline, physical fitness, a sense of belonging, and global travel, the military may be just the ticket to a more fulfilling lifestyle.

Although military salaries are generally less competitive than their civilian counterparts, there is no denying the superiority of government benefits. When evaluating the salary schedules, don't forget about the housing and food allowances, health and life insurance, education reimbursement, student loan payoffs, thirty days paid vacation per year, and military discounts on a wide spectrum of goods and services. Additional recruitment bonuses may also be available. Finally, if you join in time to serve for twenty years, the military pension and retirement plan can take a significant weight off of your future.

The main difference between joining the military as a typical enlistee just out of high school and joining as a seasoned professional is likely to be in your initial rank. If you already have a college degree, you are already at an advantage, and can expect to enlist and go straight through to officer training. Depending on your specific background and specialization, officers enjoy higher pay and occasionally more say in their career direction than enlisted recruits.

Risks in Peace and War

Aside from the obvious risks to health and safety that accompany a career transition into the military during times of war, there are also multiple peacetime risks you could face.

For the majority of specialties, serving in times of peace is no less dangerous than serving in times of war. This is due to the fact that a significant amount of time is spent preparing for war and training exercises involve live munitions and real equipment.

For example, on a Navy aircraft carrier, the main difference between peace- and wartime maneuvers is felt primarily by the pilots; either they're attempting to land a plane on an airstrip in the middle of an ocean, or they're attempting to land a plane on an airstrip in the middle of an ocean while being fired upon. Even under normal conditions, the pilots must attempt to land their planes on a platform rolling on a hostile sea, often in the dead of night. For other crew members, aircraft carriers are just as dangerous during peacetime as they are during war (and in fact are often rated the most hazardous of all places to work) due in part to their tight quarters.

Of course, there is always the chance that war or a dangerous conflict may break out suddenly. Prior to 9/11, very few people had anticipated the possibility of attacks on U.S. soil and a global war on terrorism. It's impossible to predict when the next power-hungry demagogue will surface and try to assert himself on the world stage.

Another risk is the chance of deployment to areas that are neither war zones nor particularly dangerous but that may involve an elevated risk of harm due to local politics. Since military bases are hardly inconspicuous, they make easy targets for members of extremist or separatist movements in otherwise peaceful countries. This is an important consideration for those with children who may be attending military schools on base as well, since they may face increased risk of harm or kidnapping.

A less dramatic (although more probable) type of risk is to your primary relationship. Military careers often involve long absences, beginning with the basic training you must undergo when you first sign on. Whether or not you are deployed in a war zone, not all tours of duty can accommodate taking your family along, at least not initially. Can your mate handle prolonged absences, with sometimes limited communication? Can you?

Army, Navy, or Air Force?

While to the civilian observer "the military" exists as a unified and somewhat intimidating monolith, the truth is that each of the five branches has not only a distinct mission, but a distinct personality as well.

Age Requirements

The eligibility requirements also differ considerably, with the Marine Corps and the Coast Guard having maximum age limits that make them unlikely choices for those pursuing second careers later in life.

Between the remaining three branches, the Army will take the oldest recruits (you must be no older than forty-two by the time you complete the nine- to ten-week basic-training period). In contrast, the Navy and Air Force will only accept candidates up to age thirty-five, although the Air Force will make some exceptions for high-demand specializations (such as physicians, nursing, and allied health).

Choice of Destination

The Navy will allow you to choose either the Pacific or the Atlantic for your assignment, but other than that, don't expect to have any say regarding your first tour of duty. Chances are good you'll spend a good portion of your time at sea (it is the Navy, after all!). The other branches don't offer any choices regarding destination and make no promises about where you'll go.

Job Specializations

When it comes to variety, the Army has the largest number of Military Occupational Specialties, with over 200 categories. It is followed by the Air Force with over 150 and the Navy with over 100.

The Air Force has the most specific website about the different career tracks one can take: flight, nontechnical, technical, and specialty. Technical career paths include manpower, personnel, security, and intelligence. Specialty careers include chaplain officer, band officer, and JAG (judge advocate officer). Most second-career paths are likely to fall under the nontechnical careers, which include jobs from aircraft maintenance to administrative positions.

The Navy's website offers personality and interest assessments you can take to help you decide among the various choices it offers. (You can also visit *www.military.com* and fill out a checklist based on your interests that will compare jobs across the branches.)

Pay Scale

All branches share the same basic benefits: pay, health care, retirement plan, and basic education benefits. Aside from other special compensation (such as sea pay, or hazardous duty pay) an E-1 in the Navy makes the same as his or her counterpart in the Army, Marine Corps, etc. That said, there are other incentives that may be offered to entice the potential recruit, and these will differ by branch. These include enlistment bonuses, additional educational benefits, advanced pay grade, etc.

Making the Right Choice

To get a better feel of which branch of the service is best for you, ask your recruiter if you can speak to someone who has recently joined. Second, you should also arrange to visit a nearby base and tour the facilities. (Your reaction to this environment will go a long way toward determining your compatibility with this type of career.) Finally, talk to friends and family who are currently serving in the military. Avoid asking questions of individuals who have been out of the military for some time, since they probably do not have an understanding of "today's" military. Also, avoid people who left the military under less than desirable conditions, since their opinions will tend to be tainted.

PITFALLS AND PERILS A military career, while extremely rewarding for the candidate with the right motivation and mindset, is not for everyone. There are several potentially negative aspects to a career in the military that you should carefully evaluate before embarking on a career change of this type.

First and foremost is the fact that you will have very little (if any) determination in where you will be living and working. While your first assignment may not be as dramatic as a deployment to a war zone, a move to a place you'd never considered living before could prove very traumatic for your spouse and family.

Another peril is that you may not be able to adapt to the military mindset. A successful career in the military requires a person with a profound respect for order and discipline, and who does not mind being on the receiving end of both. In addition, this mindset is often extended to the spouses of those in the service. Your spouse may not do well seeing you in such a deferent role and may not be able to adjust. Military wives also have expectations placed upon them based on their husband's rank, and your wife may not be up to the task.

On a personal level, you should be prepared for a loss of involvement in decision-making, limitations to freedom and opportunity, and a poorer level of accommodation or work environment than you've grown used to in the civilian world.

Should you ever face the need for counseling, you should know that there is a stigma in the armed forces associated with psychological problems, partly due to a military culture that often views mental illness as a sign of personal and professional weakness.

Finally, you should understand that just because you are trained in a certain specialty, you may not end up performing that task at all times. Frank, a career Navy communicator, was surprised to find himself manning a riverboat during his deployment to Vietnam instead of the radio waves. ●

SUCCESS STORY

In October of 1998, Joe was forty-six when he decided to embark on a major career change: He decided to join the Army. A successful oral and maxillofacial surgeon in private practice, his decision at first stunned his colleagues and friends. After all, he'd had no prior military service or background. "My wife wasn't even sure I'd be able to pass the physical exam," he shares.

Still, Joe listened to his own heart and picked up the phone to call a recruiter. That decision has been one he and his family have never questioned or regretted. "Not even once," he says.

You may be wondering, what would have led a successful surgeon to want to join the military? According to Joe, there were several reasons. First, the small town they were living in wasn't really providing enough of a clientele to fully fund all three of the practice's partners. As a result, he and his family had been considering a move of some type anyway.

Second, he'd long harbored the desire to give his kids the benefit of an overseas education. His colleagues responded to this explanation with, "I make enough money to take my kids to Europe any time I want." "They just didn't get it," says Joe. "There is a big difference between visiting a place and really getting ingrained in a different culture. I wanted my kids to have that experience."

Third, Joe was ready for a change from owning a practice. "One thing I realized early on is that it's impossible to really leave a practice behind," he shares. "When you get to your vacation spot, the first thing you have to do is check your messages to make sure things are still going according to plan, that the lights will still be on when you get back."

So when Joe picked up the phone and called the Army recruiter, he said, "I'm an oral surgeon and was wondering if you needed one." There was a pause before the recruiter replied, "Who is this really?" The reason for the recruiter's disbelief was simple: The Army had just decided that their number one goal for the coming year was to locate and recruit oral surgeons!

Joe's first questions were easy to answer, "Where can I go? What can I do?" The recruiter treated his questions honestly, telling him, "I can't promise you anything about where you'll go. If you want to go to Hawaii, the best we may be able to offer you is a Hawaiian shirt." However, the recruiter did tell him that someone with his degrees and specialization would come in with at least a captain's commission, "and possibly as a major." Anything beyond that would have to be seen. In addition to the direct ascension to officer status, there was also a small signing bonus and a four-year commitment.

Prior to making his decision, Joe was allowed the opportunity to chat with "one of the consultants to the Surgeon General, an oral surgeon." The consultant spent time outlining the various responsibilities and expectations Joe would have in his new career.

Once he made his decision, Joe started his physical conditioning, working out with the retired Army husband of one of his wife's friends. "He didn't know much about maxillofacial surgery, but he sure knew the beans and bullets of the Army. He helped me get in shape and understand what would be in store."

Like all new recruits, Joe was required to go to basic training. Unlike most new recruits, he entered as a lieutenant colonel. After that, his first post was a local one. This worked out for the family's needs because his wife was able to get a job working for a local high school (using her degree in library sciences). It was now 1999.

When considering a career change to the military, Joe offers this advice: "The civilian world and the military world each have good parts and bad parts. The question is, Which of the bad parts can you deal with easier?" For Joe, the answer is easy. True, he's had to sacrifice some personal freedom by joining the military; he can't just get up and go when he pleases. But he also doesn't have the weight of a practice always hanging over every decision.

What he likes best about his work in the military is that "the military is not money-driven. I don't have to make patient care decisions based on money or on a patient's ability to pay." Joe also relishes not having to clear patient care decisions through insurance companies, whose employees often have no clue about what he's talking about, instead basing their decisions "on what's included on their preprinted list."

When asked what his most rewarding moment was, Joe replies, "Getting deployed." Shortly after the 9/11 attacks, Joe was sent to serve in Uzbekistan for eight months. The experience led him to fully appreciate the lifestyle Americans enjoy at home. He shared this with his kids. "Look at this picture of this guy with a goat," he'd say. "That goat is all this guy has in the whole world." That appreciation for what they have has become ingrained in the family's values.

Joe and his family did eventually make it to their desired post in Europe. After his deployment, he was stationed at Landstuhl Army Base in Germany. During his time at Landstuhl, Joe applied his oral surgery skills to reconstructing the faces of those returning from Afghanistan and Iraq. This marked quite a change from his earlier days "working on fifteen-year-old kids with impacted wisdom teeth."

Joe says that as an officer, especially a medical officer, he is "pretty autonomous. You can pick and choose your assignments and what's right for your family." For example, he and his family have recently moved back stateside and are living in Colorado Springs. He expects this post to last long enough to see his son through college. "The Army likes to stabilize families," he shares. "They wouldn't move us when one of the kids is a junior in high school."

When asked how his family reacted to the lifestyle change, Joe says, "the kids absolutely grieved coming back stateside. My son got to argue a case on the floor of the Kremlin for the model U.N. How can you beat that?"

It's now been ten years since Joe picked up the phone and called the Army recruiter. It's a call everyone concerned is glad he made. ●

A Further Option:
Civilian Service with the Military

If you love the idea of serving in the armed forces but are limited by age, physical condition, or are geographically rooted in a specific area, you can still pursue a civilian career within the services.

Each of the branches posts career openings on the website *www.usa jobs.com*. The benefits of working for the Federal Government are excellent and include quality health insurance, a generous leave and holiday schedule, flexible and family-friendly work arrangements, long-term care insurance, and a three-part retirement program including a 401(k) type plan. In addition, salaries can be competitive and jobs are often more secure than those in the private marketplace. That said, preference for these types of jobs is most often granted to those with prior military service.

Now, let's examine the concepts we've looked at in this chapter to see if right now, you feel a military career is "worth it" to you. You may find it helpful to write down your thoughts in a notebook or to discuss these issues with your friends or family. As you answer each question, try to think of specific instances to support your opinion.

Checklist | Is It Worth It?

How many of these statements do you agree with?

○ I am completely open to serving my country in any destination the military chooses.

○ I respect and respond well to discipline.

○ I would rather follow instructions to the letter than to "think outside the box."

○ I am comfortable with the loss of autonomy inherent in a military career.

○ I am aware that in most cases, there is little difference between serving in times of peace and in times of war.

○ I am comfortable that my spouse and I can handle the added pressure from prolonged absences, dangerous assignments, and external expectations.

If there are any statements you don't agree with, now is the time to carefully analyze the reasons why and determine how much of a roadblock this item represents in your overall plan.

SUMMARY A MILITARY CAREER IS RIGHT FOR ME BECAUSE:

- I have a strong desire to serve my country.
- I am willing to adapt to a more regimented lifestyle in order to experience freedoms in different areas.
- I love the thought of traveling to different places and knowing that Uncle Sam is going to get me there!
- My spouse or family thrives on changing environments and new experiences.

CHAPTER 22

Serving a Higher Power: Religious Alternatives

As the best educated and wealthiest generation, it's not surprising that there is an increasing tendency amongst Baby Boomers to feel a calling to "do good works" as part of their second careers. As we've seen, opportunities abound for those pursuing teaching, social work, and even law enforcement careers. Increasingly, Boomers are turning to work in ministry as well.

That said, there is a growing need for those in ministry who are part of younger generations. If you're a younger worker, this means that you may find it easier to find work, especially as a youth pastor, or youth director. According to the Association of Theological Schools, more than 60 percent of new clerics are over thirty, and a third are over forty. Most are men, but women are making up an increasing share.

Why Heed the Calling

Some individuals feel a calling from an early age to enter ministry. For others, it's not unusual to begin to question the value of one's contributions upon entering your twilight years. That's why for older career changers, monetary gain often ranks second or even third behind doing work with a purpose. This is especially true for Boomers, many of whom have spent the first half of their lives acquiring material wealth and possessions.

A decision to pursue a career change to ministry represents more than just a desire to do good works. Rather, this type of career change should be undertaken only by those who feel "called" to do so. Pastoral work can be very challenging as well as rewarding, and many people will be looking to you for strength and guidance. You need to be sure that the foundation for their expectations—your faith—is strong.

Types of Seminaries

Regardless of which faith system you're part of, the typical steps involve attending seminary school, followed or complemented by some type of internship. Prior to being assigned your own congregation, you'll most likely be assisting another pastor/rabbi with their ministry before having the chance to lead one of your own.

Admission into a seminary typically requires a four-year degree (of any type) with a GPA of 2.7 or higher. Exceptions are sometimes made for individuals who only have some college but who have significant prior ministry experience.

Since seminary courses can be quite intensive, most students stretch the two-year degree out to three or more years, even if they are devoting themselves to study full-time. These days, it's also increasingly common to find students attending seminary part-time as they maintain their current careers.

For example, Fuller Theological Seminary offers an "MA in a Day" program, which offers students the chance to attend classes for one combined afternoon and evening per week (in addition to some summer intensives each year). Students can graduate with a master's in divinity in three years on this part-time format. Fuller is accredited by the Association of Theological Schools and covers one hundred Christian denominations.

While many legitimate seminaries do offer online courses, you should be aware that there are also several online "diploma mills" offering ministry degrees that will not be valid at traditional churches or synagogues.

There are actually three types of seminaries: denominational, university-related, and independent. Denominational seminaries exist to serve the needs of a particular group, whereas university-related seminaries cover multiple denominations and often exist alongside other professional schools, such as law or medicine. Independent seminaries are a newer phenomenon, but may not be recognized by the church of your choice.

The best way to find the right program is to schedule a meeting with your current pastor or rabbi and ask for a personal recommendation.

Full-Time or Bi-Vocational Ministry?

For those wishing to plunge right in, attending seminary full-time followed by a full-time position in ministry is the typical path. If you're under thirty, this might be the best option for you. If you already have an established career—and the usual accompanying responsibilities (such as a mortgage)—it may make sense to maintain your current employment while pursuing seminary part-time. Once you complete seminary, you can work in ministry part-time until you're ready to make the transition.

According to the Finisher's Project (an organization devoted to promoting mission and ministry work around the world), "There is currently a great need for this kind of self-supporting ministry. Since many established churches have grown smaller, and as new churches are just starting up, there is an increasing need for ministers who are primarily self-supporting, but who can do ministry well while still working at another job." This career path is "bi-vocational ministry."

It's not uncommon for people to choose a bi-vocational path for ten or twenty years, perhaps never even choosing to make the transition to full-time ministering before retirement.

Serving God and Country

Another growing opportunity is to work as a military chaplain. Army chaplains can either serve full-time active duty or part-time as a civilian chaplain for local reserve units. Active-duty chaplains earn much higher salaries and have better (earthly) benefits than their civilian counterparts, but the "requirements and the stakes are also significantly greater," according to the Army recruitment website. Those who enlist as active duty chaplains go straight from their military chaplain training to their staff assignment, and are not issued weapons.

PITFALLS AND PERILS Perhaps the most common pitfall for a career in ministry is a feeling of isolation. While religious leaders are often surrounded by people, they are also held apart from them. This is true both from an internal and an external perspective. Those in ministry, although human, have a higher set of expectations placed upon them. In particular, those who go to them for spiritual leadership don't always want to acknowledge their "human" side; meaning that they never want to see them with their guard down.

From an internal perspective, those in ministry are aware of this expectation, and thus can find themselves with no human counterpart to turn to in times of personal crisis or doubt. It's somewhat easier for those who are married, although spouses of religious leaders can also find themselves the objects of public scrutiny.

Being single and a pastor can pose its own problems. A pastor who chooses to date often feels undue pressure to "move to the next step" if the dates haven't been a total disaster. Some pastors report being constantly told, "We need to find you a wife," as if they are less than whole if they are single. Others say parishioners find it difficult to relate to them if they are not married or if they don't have kids.

Another pitfall of ministry work is the fact that as a spiritual counselor, you will be taking on the weight and burden of other people's problems. A lot of other people. Looking out at a congregation, it might sometimes seem that there's nothing but a sea of problems looking back at you. Those who choose this line of work need to understand that they are not meant to actually solve all of the problems they come into contact with, but rather are there to guide others to a spiritual resolution as an intermediary.

Finally, sometimes those involved in ministry can fall into a trap of feeling like they are above everyone else, answering only to God. This can lead to dangerous rationalizations when it comes to personal behavior, control of finances, and misuse of power. ●

SUCCESS STORY

While for some people it takes a lifetime to hear the calling, David knew he wanted to be a Catholic priest from the age of seven. Answering the call was another question entirely. Instead, he followed a more traditional path, going to college, getting married, and becoming a college professor at a large community college.

But the flame hadn't been extinguished entirely. "My first wife and I were expecting our first child and I had convinced her that the time had come to get involved in a church again. She agreed and we joined a parish that had a ton of kids. The senior pastor, very shortly after we joined, invited me to become an elder and that rekindled the desire to enter the ministry."

Unfortunately, David and his wife soon grew apart. She left the church and David to pursue her own interests. Meanwhile, the desire to feed his spirit and get involved in ministry only grew stronger. Rather than follow the traditional path through seminary school, David took an alternate route "which involved a very convoluted process." He found himself commuting to Wisconsin from Arizona over the summer for four years, taking classes by extension and working thirty hours per week as an associate to the pastor.

"After ten years of service I was allowed to apply for the pastoral colloquy of my denomination. Independent of that process, I elected to pursue a doctor of ministry degree, finding a program that would admit me without the traditional preparation." David completed the degree just after he was ordained a pastor in the Lutheran Church.

David's nontraditional approach allowed him to keep going with his regular full-time employment, which served not only his own financial needs, but also the needs of the church.

Since he was able to keep his teaching pension, he was able to engage in part-time ministry for many years for churches that could not afford a full-time minister. This wasn't as easy as it may sound. Like most churches without a full-time pastor, the community was not tightly knit and suffered from personality conflicts and power struggles. "It was very hard to balance a full-time teaching job, and part-time work with a very dysfunctional parish."

Today, David is the head pastor of his own church. He has no regrets whatsoever about his career change, nor about the way he went about it. The only thing he wishes he'd known before becoming involved in the process was "how nasty the Church can be, especially to their own." David often finds himself in conflict with what church leaders think is "right for the denomination." For example, he continues to participate in a three-day spiritual retreat (known as Cursillo) that is technically forbidden by his church's leadership. Rules and regulations are beside the point to him. He and his new wife are more interested in being "active, visible, and joyful witnesses for Christ." ●

An Alternative Spiritual Path

For those with a strong spiritual inclination, but not necessarily a calling to be a minister, opportunities abound for other ways to be involved. Sites such as *www.finishers.org* offer the chance to search for teaching, mission, and other types of charitable work with a spiritual component. You should also check with your local parish or synagogue.

Now, let's examine the concepts we've looked at in this chapter to see if right now, you feel a career in ministry is "worth it" to you. You may find it helpful to write down your thoughts in a notebook or to discuss these issues with your friends or family. As you answer each question, try to think of specific instances to support your opinion.

Checklist | Is It Worth It?
How many of these statements do you agree with?

○ I understand that the life of a spiritual leader can at times be lonely.

○ I am willing to live my life in a transparent fashion.

○ I am comfortable knowing that as a religious leader, I will face elevated expectations from those in my congregation and community.

○ My spouse is comfortable dealing with changes in the way others perceive us.

SUMMARY A CAREER IN MINISTRY IS RIGHT FOR ME BECAUSE:

• I feel God is calling me.
• I am strong in my faith.
• I have a love for other people and a desire to help them.
• I am willing to live my life in a way that puts God first.

CHAPTER 23

Acting Locally: Public Policy and Political Positions

For those who have already had fulfilling careers, the next logical progression is often a strong inclination to "give back" to one's local community. Those who've experienced success in their first careers often have the right combination of education, income, and self-confidence needed for a career in public policy.

Grass-Roots Versus National or International Organizations

If you're passionate about an issue, the best place to roll up your sleeves and get to work is on a local level. The slogan "Think globally, act locally" is not without merit. Most people, however, tend to stop at the "think globally" part. The trouble with this approach is that problems can appear insurmountable at a macro level, leading to feelings of frustration and a tendency to give up. For example, try thinking about how you can stop world hunger, and then compare that feeling to what you can do about the hungry in your own community. What can you contribute to the fight against global warming? Compare that to what can be done about controlling emissions in your own town. Everyone knows that HIV and AIDS are major issues internationally, but do you know what the statistics are for these diseases in your town's teen population?

Once you recognize the power for change one person can have on a local level, you may consider doing more than sending your favorite charity an annual contribution. Maybe it's time to devote that most precious of your resources, your time, to making a difference for a cause you truly believe in.

The same thing is true of political parties. If you strongly support a specific party's platform, there is much more you can do besides turning out to vote in the presidential elections every four years. The major parties all report a need for volunteers at the community level. Our nation's leaders, after all, are often plucked from the ranks of those successful on a local level.

If your ultimate goal is a political position with a national or international organization, it's important to first build your experience by either working or volunteering on the local level. If you've already built your resume, you should also work on your knowledge base, by taking courses in political science and economics. Foreign policy is also helpful.

Once you have the knowledge base and the experience, you're ready to approach national (or international organizations). Visit the companion website for links.

Making a Difference in Your Own Community

Voting turnout for local elections can be as low as 1 percent in small towns; most people don't realize that the vast majority of the laws that govern them are created on a local level. The water you drink, the air you breathe, the roads you drive on, your town's amenities, the medical services available to you, the quality of the education your children receive, the wages you earn, the value of your house, and the crime in your neighborhood are all impacted by local decision-makers. Does that make you more inclined to attend your next City Council meeting?

If you want to get involved in local politics, that's actually a pretty good place to start. According to Dr. Harry Crisp, currently serving a term on the Stafford County, Virginia, Board of Supervisors, "It's important to attend these kinds of meetings so you can really understand the local issues." It's also the best place to make connections, and politics is all about networking. "The best thing to do is volunteer for a committee. There are lots of choices: parks and recreation, planning and zoning, agriculture. These committees are always looking for volunteers."

John Gallen, two-time city councilman for Copperas Cove, Texas, started his journey in local politics on the City Board of Adjustments. "We primarily worked with variances to city ordinances," he says, which gave him a solid understanding of the intricacies of his town's regulations. From there, he was invited to work on the town Planning and Zoning Committee. After that, he ran for City Council twice and served two three-year terms. Today, he's back on the Planning and Zoning committee as he contemplates a third term.

We'll learn from both Harry and John's experiences in the next few sections.

PITFALLS AND PERILS As anyone who has campaigned for and served in public office will tell you: Campaigning is a far cry from governing. Even those with the best intentions end up making promises on the campaign trail that they can't possibly keep. This is the one of the most frustrating issues for new legislators, and there are many reasons for it. For one thing—as illustrated in Harry Crisp's story—you'll often serve with other people who've been elected on promises directly opposed to those you made. For another, just getting certain initiatives on a ballot can be difficult. There simply isn't enough room to vote on every issue that every citizen has, and legislators frequently have to choose between serving those who helped them get elected and the needs of the population at large.

John Gallen adds, "The old adage that 'Politics makes strange bed fellows' is totally true." John admits he was "steamrolled" twice by people he trusted, but ended up becoming good friends with two of the men he ran against. "Being able to read people is truly the key to a successful career in politics," he says.

Campaigning for office is extremely time-consuming, and physically and mentally draining. In addition, there is always the chance for campaigns to get ugly, so you have to be really dedicated to decide to run for office.

Not only must you be ready to face these issues, but your spouse and family must as well. Campaigns don't have to get ugly to strain your relationships. After watching him lose twice, one politician's wife really didn't want him to run again for fear of how disappointed he would be. As a result, she actually read about his intention to run again in the paper. "That's not an approach I would recommend," he chuckles.

Once you've spent considerable resources campaigning to get elected, you should know that stipends for public servants are usually nowhere near the full-time salaries you probably enjoyed in your prior career and are usually not enough to live on. Most people in these positions are either retired with pensions or have other paying jobs or consultancies as well. If the latter is the case for you, you'll need to be careful that there is no chance of conflict of interest between your careers.

If you're not interested in holding an elected office, but rather are more interested in a civil service position, you should be aware that these jobs can be very difficult to attain for newcomers. If you're a member of a protected class (disabled or a veteran), it will be easier. Otherwise, you'll have to work hard to sell your prior experience in the corporate sector. If you can get in, however, the salaries and benefits make it worth the effort. ●

SUCCESS STORY

Despite a strong shared interest with his wife Bobby in state and national politics, Dr. Harry Crisp had no intention of entering local politics. One day, a message on his home answering machine changed all of that. "Harry, we heard Pete Fields isn't going to run for the Board of Supervisors this year. A bunch of us talked it over, and we think you're the man for the job." Harry and Bobby just looked at each other, stunned. "I didn't have any thought in my mind of doing this at all," he shares. After talking it over with his wife, several of their friends, and the local Democratic Party, they decided to go for it. "We approached the entire process as a team," he says.

With a doctorate in electrical engineering, Harry had spent thirty-three years working for the U.S. Navy and for the local electric power company. Some of this experience was directly relevant. "Even in the systems engineering world, there's a certain amount of politics involved. You have exposure to that." In engineering, however, one is guided by a specific scientific foundation. "There are certain principles you can't violate." In politics, things aren't so black and white.

At the time he received that voice mail message, Harry was just finishing up a two-year term on his local parish council while working as an engineering consultant part-time. "I'd been looking forward to a whole lot of golf and fishing," he says. It was not to be. As it turns out, though, he did get quite a bit of exercise . . . knocking on doors—4,500 doors, to be exact. "I lost fifteen pounds while campaigning." He adds, "I'm probably in the best shape I've ever been in."

Campaigning was hard work: After a big kickoff event, there was a lot of mailing, planning, and organizing to be done. "It was an incredibly interesting and challenging experience. Rewarding, even if you don't win." Harry says he felt really enriched by the process of "getting out there and interacting with the citizens, exchanging views with a whole lot of people who are deeply interested in their community, the future, and the welfare of everyone."

Naturally, there were rough days, too, when he felt he hadn't accomplished much, or when he felt he was all alone. "Those were the days I sometimes questioned my decision." Usually, a good night's sleep offered a fresh perspective, and the next day would start out with a renewed sense of purpose and energy. Harry campaigned door-to-door from August all the way up to Election Day in November.

One of the people Harry met while knocking on doors was an eighty-one-year-old widow. Her husband had long operated a business out of their home, which as a result had been zoned as commercial property. Although he'd died ten years earlier, she had never petitioned to change her property's status because she had never had to pay taxes on it. (There was an automatic property tax exclusion for those sixty-five and older and the disabled.) Thanks to recent changes in the tax structure, the widow now found herself faced with a gigantic property tax bill. On a fixed income of $500 a month from Social Security, there was no way she could pay it. Harry promised her he would look into it if he got elected.

His hard work paid off with more than just weight loss and interesting conversations: Harry was elected to a four-year term on the Stafford County Board of Supervisors. He didn't forget his campaign promise to the widow. "We interacted with the county government to rezone her property back to residential status. It reduced the value sufficiently for her to not pay taxes."

That success aside, Harry shares that campaigning for office is one thing, while governing is another. "When you're campaigning for office, you have a vision of what you want to do. Making that happen is really an art." He says that in order to be an effective legislator, "You really have to use every single skill you have: persuasion, communication, and relying on other people to achieve your objectives. Personalities become the major challenge." In addition, says Harry, "You've got to interact with other members of the board, some of whom may be equally passionate about conflicting interests."

Despite the challenges, Harry is happy he answered the call to local politics. For one thing, it's afforded him and his wife the chance to really make a difference in areas they were already passionate about, such as protecting the rural and historic areas from urban sprawl. A member of the Daughters of the American Revolution, Bobby can trace her ancestors back to the Mayflower, while Harry can trace his to the Revolutionary War. Consequently, they've both been passionate about preserving historical sites. "Now that I'm in office, I do have an opportunity to impact that," he says, through a new comprehensive plan for the county. "We are directing growth into the areas where we already have schools, roads, and public safety while preserving open spaces."

Harry's advice for those interested in a career in public politics is simply, "Do the best job you can to provide services for your community's residents. You have the power to impact a lot of people in a positive way." ●

A career in public politics or working for a cause-related organization can be one of the most rewarding choices you can make. The work you'll do will be challenging, but the impact will be substantial and oftentimes affect many generations.

Opportunities in public service exist for city council members, mayors, city commissioners, township trustees, election administrators, school superintendents, treasurers, and more. If you're interested in working for your local government, call them up and ask what opportunities might be coming available for someone with your expertise.

Cause-related organizations include historical preservation societies, local environmental lobbies, organizations for the homeless, antipoverty initiatives, programs to fight illiteracy, and drug and alcohol abuse treatment programs. You can also get involved in educational campaigns for HIV and AIDS and cancer prevention.

Now, let's examine the concepts we've looked at in this chapter to see if right now, you feel a career in politics is "worth it" to you. You may find it helpful to write down your thoughts in a notebook or discuss these issues with your friends or family. As you answer each question, try to think of specific instances to support your opinion.

Checklist | Is It Worth It?

How many of these statements do you agree with?

○ Political campaigns can be emotionally and physically exhausting, but my beliefs are strong enough to see me through.

○ My family is prepared to weather a potentially stormy campaign.

○ I am good at reading people and knowing whom to trust, but I am prepared to be cautious regarding my relationships.

○ I don't have a tendency to take things personally.

○ I understand that stipends for public servants (at the local level) are often quite low.

If there are any statements you don't agree with, now is the time to carefully analyze the reasons why and determine how much of a roadblock this item represents in your overall plan.

SUMMARY A CAREER IN PUBLIC SERVICE OR POLITICS IS RIGHT FOR ME BECAUSE:

- I have strong beliefs about specific issues that I would like to do something about.
- My interpersonal skills, educational background, and work experience are perfect for a career in politics.
- I am willing to deal with the negative side of politics in order to achieve my goals.
- My family is resilient enough to support me throughout my campaign and political career.
- Rather than discussing problems on a global level, I'd rather tackle them head-on at the local level.

Conclusion:
You're On Your Way

Congratulations! Finishing this book was the first step onto the path toward a richer life, one designed around your own definition of "success." You should now be armed with a realistic self-assessment, a preliminary written roadmap leading to your goal, and a feeling of inspiration and confidence from the stories of people—just like you—who dared to take the plunge and realize their dreams. Now, it's your turn. In the words of hockey superstar Wayne Gretzky, "Procrastination is one of the most common and deadliest of diseases and its toll on success and happiness is heavy." Remember, *now* is the time to do what you love . . . so go do it!

INDEX

ABOUT THE AUTHOR

Nancy Whitney-Reiter is a former economist and corporate market analyst. After surviving the September 11 attacks on the World Trade Center, she found herself questioning the true meaning of "success." In 2003, she quit her job and sold most of her possessions to embark on a year long international travel sabbatical. The fruits of her journey are chronicled in *Unplugged: How to Disconnect from the Rat Race, Have an Existential Crisis, and Find Meaning and Fulfillment* (Sentient, 2008). She lives in Arizona with her husband, award-winning flamenco guitarist Greg Reiter.

Printed in the United States
By Bookmasters